Apple Games and Customs

Common Ground

First published by Common Ground in 1994,
reprinted 2005.

Common Ground
Gold Hill House
21 High Street
Shaftesbury
Dorset SP7 8JE

ISBN l-870364-l2-0

Text by Beatrice Mayfield
Cover design © David Holmes 2005
Designed and typeset in Times on an Apple Macintosh by
Beatrice Mayfield and Stephen Turner at Common Ground 1994.
2005 facsimile by Eco-Logic Books - www.eco-logicbooks.com
Printed by Russell Press on Cyclus Offset - 100% post
consumer waste

CONTENTS

ACKNOWLEDGEMENTS

Common Ground offers grateful thanks to Beatrice Mayfield, who never believed she could research and write a book, but here it is.

Thanks too to Sophie Grigson for weaving a thoughtful and optimistic foreword and to all the people who generously gave of their knowledge, particularly to the English Folk Dance and Song Society, The Folklore Society, Michael and Wendy Dacre, Dave Occomore, Roy Palmer, Ruth Ward and others whose work we have foraged through. Please go to them or their books, listed under References for more detail. See page 112 for formal acknowledgements.

Common Ground relies on grants and donations to continue its work. The Save Our Orchards campaign and work to promote Apple Day have been grant aided over the years by the Countryside Commission/Agency, The Department of the Environment/Defra Environmental Action Fund, The Cobb Charity, The Garfield Weston Foundation, The Lyndhurst Settlement, The Tedworth Charitable Trust and Jenny Sheridan. We are most grateful for their support and that of others.

Common Ground, charity no: 326335.

A MEMORY OF APPLES
by
Sophie Grigson

Some half dozen or so apple trees were scattered around the far end of my parents' garden. The big old ones must have been remnants of an earlier orchard, the younger trees planted by my father. My favourite, for eating that is, was the Beauty of Bath, which blushed pink against a startlingly white flesh when you bit into it. My swing hung from the branches of the sturdy, solid and massive cooking apple tree, and in spring I would fly up into a froth of white blossom, in autumn I would try to catch an apple before I dropped back down to the ground.

I don't remember the variety, but I do remember the intense sourness of those fruit - my friends and I would dare each other to bite into them, our own apple game. It became something of an autumn ritual, first kicking around the windfalls to disturb the insistent wasps and other wild life, then wincing at the sudden rush of tart cool juice, and the delighted grimaces as we victoriously swallowed enough to satisfy childish honour.

As children, we instinctively placed a greater value on apples than that of mere sustenance. We were, quite unwittingly, slotting into an ancient pattern. Apples have played an important role in British life since time immemorial. They are the quintessential British fruit. Commonplace, to be sure, but always highly and rightly valued, at least until the latter part of this century, when big business stripped away so much of their magic. Not only did we nearly lose huge numbers of the older varieties, we also nearly lost a huge chunk of our heritage.

In this last decade of the twentieth century, however, the dignity and power of the apple is being restored, thanks largely to the charity Common Ground. In 1990 I went to their first Apple Day celebration in Covent Garden. There I tasted again my childhood favourite, the Beauty of Bath, and other apples that I'd never seen in the flesh, some that I'd never even heard of before. That year, Kidd's Orange Red stood out amongst the crowds of apple varieties, for me at least.

Nowadays most people have access, to some degree, to a wider variety of British apples. City dwellers are beginning to comprehend again the essential seasonality of apples and to realise that there is a positive value to brief availability of some of the older varieties. As one reaches the end of its prime, so another steps in to take its place, right through from late summer to early winter. A natural and timely cavalcade, ensuring that the consumer never gets bored and never has to make do with second best.

With this book, Common Ground have taken up the cudgel again on behalf of our best beloved fruit. In the gentlest of senses, of course, but with the quiet determination that they know succeeds. Here, you will find an extraordinary collection of traditional and reinvented apple games and customs, as well as old rhymes that record much of our small scale, domestic and social history.

Everyone knows that an apple a day keeps the doctor away, and most people still associate apple bobbing and toffee apples with Hallowe'en. These are familiar nation-wide, but it's the local traditions that are in greatest peril of oblivion. As small orchards have been destroyed to make way for housing estates or new roads or whatever, the ceremonies connected to them for centuries have dis-appeared too. Wassailing and Catterning songs, for instance, were once widely spread and individual, often containing local place names and references. Now they are barely remembered, and too rarely sung.

It's not just a rural pre-occupation either. Apple trees grow in cities too, and city-dwellers have appreciated a good apple just as much as any one else. "Orange and lemons" said the bells of St. Clements, but did you remember that the bells of Whitechapel said "two sticks and an apple"?[1] Or indeed, have you ever come across this rhyme:

> Upon Paul's steeple stands a tree
> As full of apples as may be.

> The little boys of London town
> They run with hooks to pull them down;
> And then they run from hedge to hedge
> Until they come to London Bridge.[2]

It's an old, old rhyme, long before the Great Fire of 1666, St. Paul's did have a steeple, but it was destroyed by lightning in 1561.

These kinds of traditions – rhymes, songs, rituals – provide an essential link with our history, playing us tantalising hints of the lives of our forebears. They remind us that though much may have changed, a good deal of it for the better, there are still common elements which time cannot erode. The simple pleasures in life are not so very different now -a bite of a crisp, juicy apple, apple pie with cream, a stroll through a blossoming apple orchard, the changing seasons. These are things that we can share and celebrate with the generations that came before us.

AN APPLE FOR THE FUTURE
by
Sue Clifford and Angela King

The apple is the tool of the fortuneteller. It has been our most popular and commonplace fruit for hundreds of years, and our relationship with it is profound. But unless we all work hard to fight the forces of standardization and homogenization we foresee the loss of our traditional orchards and all the cultural associations that go with them.

We are all implicated, we can all do something. It can be as demanding as saving an old orchard from development, creating a community orchard, helping plan a school, hospital or city orchard, or building celebration back into the locality. It can be as simple as buying local apples in season, cooking with named varieties (a sister volume, "The Apple Source Book" offers particular recipes for diverse apples), and playing apple games.

Common Ground has been working to encourage people to save traditional orchards and the hundreds of varieties of apple that we can grow here, in many different ways.

Apple Day, initiated by Common Ground on October 21st 1990, is an annual celebration of the richness of the apple and the orchard. Within ten years Apple Day was being organised in over 600 places by village halls, Lloyd's of London, County and District Councils, schools, the National Trust, museums, juice producers, apple growers, cider makers, farmers, nurserymen, doctor's surgeries, bakers, restaurants, wildlife trusts, arts centres, agricultural and horticultural colleges, the Houses of Parliament and school meals services. From Stirling to Truro, people are inventing or rediscovering ways of sharing produce and knowledge, while enjoying themselves.

The hundreds of customs and games that we have created around the apple, echo the importance it has had in our lives. Almost every farm had its orchard, labourers were paid in cider, city folk travelled to pick fruit miles from home, costermongers' cries rang out in street markets, greengrocers put out baths of water for games of duck apple at Hallowe'en.

Levity has grown out of hard work and long knowledge. It takes time for customs to differentiate themselves, just as an intricate landscape demonstrates the deep relationship which we and nature have developed over hundreds of years. Games and customs can help us to learn from each other and by bringing us into enjoyable social contact, they also help to hold a culture together and reinforce local identity.

Orchards are very different from place to place. In Shropshire damson trees march along the hedgerows, as do cherries in parts of Norfolk. Orchards of giant cherry trees, 60 feet high, characterize the north Kent coast, while cob nut plats pick out the ragstone soils in the Weald. Hereford, Somerset and Devon are renowned for their cider apple trees, Gloucestershire for its many kinds of perry pears.

But the apple must stand for them all, with its powerful symbolism, rich poetry and its extraordinary diversity (we have grown in Britain 2,000 varieties of cooking and eating apples and some hundreds more kinds for cider). The Keswick Codlin, Yorkshire Greening, Cornish Honeypin, Monmouthshire Beauty, Tower of Glamis, Kentish Fillbasket, and Stoke Edith Pippin reveal some of the particularities of origin.

The rich repertoire of apple games and customs also links season, produce and locality, and yet we are in danger of forgetting what they mean, because we have ceased to value our apples and orchards. Whether we lose a custom or an orchard first hardly matters, the loss of either starts the fall.

When an orchard is grubbed out for agriculture or development, the loss for local distinctiveness goes deep. Of course we lose the groves, the tall trees, little ordered woods, the spring blossom bursting when all else is monotone, the shade and greens of summer, the colours and smells of autumn and the winter mistletoe.

Deprived of the richness in the landscape, we also lose the wild life: the buzz of bees working on the blossom, the thrushes, blackbirds and butterflies bargaining over fallen fruit, the hare resting under the pear tree, the wild flowers.

As the local varieties disappear so do the reliant recipes, songs, stories and customs. The ways of making cider are lost along with the skills of pruning, grafting and personally planting the land, based on generations of hard won wisdom about each variety, slope and corner. Buildings crumble having lost their use, the back breaking, but social, work falls away, neighbours become strangers.

The cultural landscape is both robust and vulnerable. Like nature it needs change to keep it in good heart, but it also needs continuity: the passing on of knowledge, an unbroken chain of care.

Our long association with apples has brought us myriad fascinating customs, sayings and songs, some are peculiar to a single village, wassailing songs vary subtly from place to place, while other pastimes and sayings are common to us all. It is worth serious effort to be true to local tradition and add new layers of meaning which reinforce local distinctiveness. This book attempts to capture the flavour of just a few of the many British games and customs around the apple, in the hope that they will not simply live on in our memory, but continue to evolve in their place.

APPLE GAMES AND CUSTOMS

Beatrice Mayfield

PART I

TRADITIONAL APPLE GAMES

Most games using apples were traditionally played at Hallowe'en, 31st October, due to their abundance at this time of year. Many of these games are still popular and continue to be enjoyed at this time of year. The importance of the apple at this festival is reflected in the alternative names given to it across the country.

Dookie Apple Night. *Newcastle*

Duck Apple Night. *Liverpool, Merseyside*

Apple and Candle Night. *Swansea, Glamorgan*

Bob Apple or Crab Apple Night. *Pontypool, Gwent* [3]

> Crab Apple Night, Is my delight.
> *Monmouthshire (Gwent)* [3]

HALLOWE'EN GAMES

Apple Bobbing, Duck Apple or Dookin' for Aipples.

> Min' hoo we dooked for aipples then?
> The traikle scones, an' ging'bread men?
> An' chestnuts roastin' in the grate
> By jumpin' oot wad tell's oor fate? [4]

Apples are floated in a tub of water, the aim is to retrieve an apple without using your hands, only your mouth. Each person is allowed three attempts, before giving up.[5] The game can be made messier and more difficult if it is played blindfold.[6] Apples of different sizes can be seen as symbols of fortune, the larger the apple caught, the greater the fortune, failure to catch an apple implies a life of poverty.[7]

In parts of Scotland after successfully ducking for an apple the first name a man heard mentioned was supposed to be that of his future wife. [7]

In Caerleon, Gwent, shops used to have an apple bobbing tub at Hallowe'en so anyone could have a go.[8]

Apple bobbing was also played in Devon and Somerset at Christmas during the lighting of the Yule Log.[9]

Fork Apple

This game is similar to Apple Bobbing, but the player holds a fork between her teeth and attempts to spear an apple floating in a tub of water.[5] Players kneel on a chair, placed with its back to the tub and try to stab an apple. Alternatively they can drop the fork by hand from a standing position and pierce an apple.[4]

> Hallowe'en is here,
> It comes but once a year,
> Apples rosy red
> Float in the water clear.
> Hold the fork on high - drop it -
> Hi! You've got a big one![4]

Apple on a string, Snap Apple or Bob Apple.
These are all names for the game where an apple is tied to a string suspended from a stick and spun round. The player

has to attempt to take a bite out of it without using their hands.[5] To make the game more competitive two or three players can attempt to eat the same apple at the same time. This game was also played with cherries.

Apple on the line
On which we must dine.
Wales [3]

Apple and candle

A string with an apple tied to one end and a candle to the other is hung from the ceiling. This is whirled round while the player tries to take a bite out of the apple, but has to avoid being splattered with hot wax or getting a mouthful of candle.[5]

Apple on the mound

This game from Cwmbran, Gwent involves placing a very small apple on top of a large mound of flour. Each player takes it turn to scoop away some of the flour without dislodging the apple. When it falls the unlucky person has to lift it clear from the flour with his mouth. In Slough, Berkshire, this game was also played using a mound of soot or salt.[3]

Pass the apple

This is played with two or more teams. Team members stand in a line with their hands behind their backs. An apple is passed along the line from chin to chin. If it is dropped then it has to start again at the beginning of the line. The winning team is the one who gets it to the end first.[10]

Apple-pie bed
A practical joke played by folding the top bed sheet in half so there isn't room to get in, or uncomfortable objects are placed in the bed and the covers smoothed over to hide them.

Apple, Plum Pudding!
A Tag game where one child is 'it', and all the other players hold onto him. 'It' calls out: Apple, plum ....! - banana, or pie, etc. If anyone lets go then they take his place. However if 'it' calls: Apple, plum pudding! Then everyone lets go and runs, 'it' chases them and tries to catch someone who becomes 'it'. Another version of this is known as Apple, plum, poison! and is played in exactly the same way.[11]

In Somerset the apple tree was sometimes seen as a sanctuary in catching games:

> Bogey, Bogey, don't catch me!
> Catch that girl in the apple tree.[12]

NEW GAMES

Most of these games have been supplied by Apple Day
organisers. They are new inventions or traditional games
adapted to have an apple theme to play on October 21st.

TAG GAMES

Gruacach's Treasure
A Gruacach was a hairy ogre in Celtic mythology.
The child playing the Gruacach lies down, pretending to be
fast asleep beside a pile of apples. The other children creep
towards her to steal the apples. If she sits up they stand stock
still. If an apple is taken the Gruacach chases after them
trying to capture anyone who has an apple before they reach
base. Anyone seen moving, or who is caught, drops out.

The Apple Tree Man and the Griggler
There is a version of Somerset folklore which believed the
Apple Tree Man lived in the oldest apple tree in the orchard
and acted as a guardian spirit. Small apples were left on the
trees after the harvest for the fairy folk or 'grigs', who were
a type of fairy. Those who stole them were known as
grigglers.
The griggler is banished while the other players form a
circle round a pile of apples. One is secretly chosen as the
Apple Tree Man. The griggler enters the circle under any

pair of arms, but he must leave under the same pair. His aim is to take an apple and escape before the Apple Tree Man can 'tag' him, but he doesn't know who to avoid. He can't be touched until he has an apple in his hand and only the Apple Tree Man can 'tag' him. He remains the griggler until he is caught, then the Apple Tree Man becomes the griggler.

Gathering Apples
Players line up at one end of a room, at the other is a row of apples, two or three less than there are players. On the word, 'Pick!' everyone dashes for an apple. Those who don't get one drop out. Two or three more are removed and the players dash again. This continues until there is only one player left who is the winner.

Apple Scramble
Different varieties of apples are scattered haphazardly on the floor, players line up at one end of the room. The name of a variety is called out and players have to race to pick one up. If a player takes the wrong variety or doesn't manage to get an apple she is out. The winner is the one who has collected the correct apples at the end of a time limit.

Orchard Looting
Teams line up facing each other at opposite ends of a room. An orchard area is drawn in front of each team and scattered with apples. Each member of the team runs in turn to his opponent's circle and collects an apple. The first team to

collect all the apples from the opponent's circle wins.

Apple Snatch

The room is divided into two barns by a base line, each occupied by a team and scattered with apples. The aim of each team is to raid the enemy's barn and steal her apples without being tagged by an opponent. If a player manages this, she may return to her own barn safely. If she is caught before securing one she is sent to prison, trapped in the enemy's barn among the apples until being freed by a member of her own side. No apples can be taken while prisoners are held. The side which steals all the apples or locks up all their opponents first wins.

PARTICIPATION GAMES

Apple and Tunnel

Two teams or more line up behind one another. An apple is passed over the head of one player and through the legs of the next. The last person in the line has to run to the front of the line with the apple. If it is dropped then the apple has to start again at the front of the line.

Apple Feat

Players sit in two rows facing one another. Each team passes an apple from one end to the other by holding it between their feet. If the apple is dropped it must be retrieved and

lifted using the feet only. The side which gets its apple from one end to the other fastest wins.

The Longest Peel Competition

This is a popular game played at many Apple Day events. The aim is to see who can make the longest peeling within the shortest time, but without it breaking. *Essington Fruit Farm, Staffordshire '92 & Kingston Maurward '93*

Hunt the apple

There are two versions of this game, the second one has been played at many Apple Day events.

1. All the players but one are sent from the room. The remaining person hides an apple out of sight. The others are allowed back in and have to find the apple as quickly as possible. The hider can help them by calling 'Ripe!'or 'Rotten!', depending on how close they are to discovering it. To make the game more frustrating she can bluff about this. The player who finds the apple first becomes the hider.

2. Apples can be hidden either inside or outside. Players have to find them from clues hidden with the apples, each

clue leads them to the next. *Cider Museum, Hereford '93 & Thornham Field Centre, Suffolk '93*

Passing the Apple
Players sit in a circle and pass an apple from one to another behind their backs in any direction. One player sits in the middle and has to guess where the apple is at a certain time. If he guesses correctly then the person holding the apple at the time takes his place.

Bowling the Apple
The aim is to bowl different varieties of apple through holes cut in a board. The size of the holes should correspond to the variety of apple. This can also be played by rolling the apple in to holes in the ground or through arches. *Middle Farm, Firle, Sussex '92 & Alderman Pounder Infants School, Notts '93*

Apple and Spoon Race
Players line up on a start line, each with an apple balanced in a spoon. Small apples such as Pitmaston Pine-Apple, which will easily sit on a wooden or tablespoon are best. The object is for players to race to a set point without dropping the apple, if they do they must retrieve it

and get it back onto the spoon, without using their hands. First across the finishing line wins her apple. *Lothian '91 & The Brandy Wharf Cider Centre, Lincolnshire '92*

Swing Apple

An apple is suspended or held by an adult before an indoor or outdoor swing. The player, starting from a still position swings himself high enough so he can either catch the apple in one hand or in his teeth. The player who is able to do this with the fewest number of back and forth swings wins.

William Tell Apple Shy

William Tell was a Swiss folk hero who shot an apple off his son's head with a bow and arrow. Knock the apple off the person's head using bean bags, water pistols or foam balls. The apple can be made from papier-mache or fabric and be larger than life. *Bromham Mill, Bedford '91*

WORD GAMES

Apple Anagrams

Anagrams have proved to be a good Apple Day game. Here are some varieties with the clues and answers.

MOT TUPT - Male cat pulls one letter off window sealant. (Cider and cooker) *TOM PUTT*

SYALD SGFERIN - Crabs poisonous parts. (Cider) *LADY'S FINGERS*

YMAERBL NELSEIGSD - Now famous variety of apple which originated in Southwell early C19. (Cooker and store) *BRAMLEY SEEDLING*

OXC - "...that crow in the morn." (Eater) *COX*

RSDVNHEOIEN RQAEDRUNE - West country county has a lion living in a stony hollow. (Eater) *DEVONSHIRE QUARRENDEN*

ENDRAIGER - Guardsman (Cooker) *GRENADIER*

CASKL AM RIDGEL - Loosen my stays (Cider) *SLACK MA GIRDLE*

DER YOLAR - Fergie!!! (Cider) *RED ROYAL*

South Hams Environment Service, Devon '93

Apple Words

Compile crosswords relating to apples, harvesting and customs with answers hidden in an apple display. *Cider Museum, Hereford '92*

Compile a word bank about apples or tastes to make a poem. *Gartmore Primary School, Stirling '92*

Apple ABC

Take a letter of the alphabet and name as many apple objects, varieties, customs, etc beginning with that letter within a set time limit.

Cooker, eater, county, colour....

A player calls out either cooker, eater, county, colour, taste or use. The next player must name an apple that fits the category named. If he does so correctly then it is his turn, if not, he loses his turn and gains a point. The first player to reach ten points is the loser.

Apple Word Squares
Find the names of different varieties or customs hidden in word squares. They could read forwards, backwards, upwards, downwards or diagonally.

Apple Scrabble
Played in the same way as ordinary Scrabble, but using only apple-related words.

Apple Hangman
Guess the variety of apple or apple-related word by calling out letters, before the man on the gallows is drawn.

GUESSING & MEMORY GAMES

True or False
One person calls out statements about apples, which if true, players flap their arms up and down, but stay still if they are false. The aim is to catch players out by tricking them into responding to false statements. Those that do are out. The game continues until there is only one player left, who then becomes the caller.

Who am I?

1) A player decides on a variety of apple or an apple-related custom, etc and provides one clue. The other players have to guess this within twenty questions, but can only ask questions that can be answered by Yes or No.

2) Each player secretly writes down an apple variety and sticks it on the forehead of the player next to her. Each person has to guess what variety it is by asking questions, which can only be answered by Yes or No.

Where am I from?

Players sit in a circle, one person tells his neighbour what variety of apple he wants to eat, that player must then state the county that variety comes from. If he does correctly then it is his turn, if not he is a rotten apple and drops out.

Apple Charades

Members of teams dress up, act out or draw either a name of an apple, custom, etc, for the other team to guess.

An Apple Play

The Somerset Apple Play by Eddie Upton was performed by Folk South West at The Brewhouse, Taunton, Somerset in 1993 as part of their Apple Day celebrations. It was based on Mummers plays and the characters were named after different varieties of apples.

Write your own play or story using apple characters. Look at different varieties, think about their colour, shape and taste and imagine what sort of personalities they would have if they were people.

Guess the Variety

Players are blindfolded and given an apple. From the smell, feel and taste they have to guess the variety.

I went to market

"I went to market and bought a ...." variety of apple, which can either be arbitrary or players can go through the letters of the alphabet. Each player has to recite all those already mentioned and then add one of their own.

Apple Happy Families

Families are made up by tracing the lineage of one apple back through those that were crossed to make it, the parent apples, and then parent varieties. For example: Discovery comes from a cross between Beauty of Bath and Worcester Pearmain, which comes from Devonshire Quarrenden. Each family is made up of four cards, and is played in the same way as traditional Happy Families. Make cards by drawing the apple varieties or printing them.

Apple Snap

The cards can either be decorated with apple prints, by halving an apple either way, as each variety makes its own unique mark, or draw different varieties. Make sure there is an even number of each card. The cards are divided equally between two or more players. Each takes it in turns to place a card face upwards in the middle of the table. When two of the same cards are put down the first player to shout 'Apple Snap' wins all the cards and the game begins again.

Apple Pairs
The same cards for apple snap can be used. The whole pack is spread face downwards. Players take it in turns to turn over any two cards, if they are not a pair they must be turned back over again. The aim is to collect as many pairs by remembering the position of cards.

Pin the maggot on the apple
Make a large paper apple with a small maggot hole somewhere on it and a maggot to match. Players are blindfolded and spun round. The aim is for them to pin the maggot on his hole. Other versions: pin the stalk or the leaf on the apple; pin the apple on a branch on a tree; pin the pip on an apple.

Apple Map
Draw an outline map of the British Isles. Make drawings of different varieties of apples and cut them out. Shuffle the apples and give one to each player. The aim is to pin the apple in its place of origin.

Common Ground's county Apple Map will help with many of these games.

PAPER & DRAWING GAMES

Consequences

The first player draws the leaves and stalk of an apple and folds the paper over so their drawing is out of sight. The next player draws the top third of an apple and folds it over, the next the middle, and the next the bottom part. To invent an especially extraordinary apple, colour each section as well.

Tangram

Each player has a different variety of apple made out of paper or card which have been cut into abstract shapes, and muddled up. The aim is to recreate the apple as quickly as possible. To make it more difficult all the pieces from the different apples can be shuffled and put in a pool in the middle of the table.

Apple Dice

An apple can be split up into six parts, each one corresponding with a number on a dice. The cheek or outline = 6, the stalk = 5, the eye = 4, the core line = 3, two cells = 2, four pips = 1. The aim is to draw the cross section of the apple by throwing the dice. To start players must throw a six to draw an outline, the pips can not be drawn until last, but the other parts can be added in any order.

MAKING APPLE OBJECTS

Apple Dolls

"Loose Feet" were dolls with a carved dried apple for a head and a body of wrapped corn husks made by the North American Seneca Indians. The doll was a very kind, happy spirit, very old and wise, who granted small children their wishes.

To make the head; peel an apple, leaving the stalk and surrounding skin. Smallish round apples work best, such as Cox's Orange Pippin, Lord Burghley or Tydeman's Late Orange. Shape the face with a spoon or knife, cutting indentations for eyes and into cheeks to form a nose. Dip the whole apple into lemon juice to stop it turning brown. Hang in an airy place for a few days or a warm oven over night and watch the face develop as it dries and shrinks. Once it is completely dry shape by pinching or snipping.

For the body, take a 24" length of thin wire twisted together for about 6", then spread into two legs. A 10" length of wire is inserted about 3" from the top of the legs to form the arms. The loop of wire above the arms is cut so it can be separated into 2" and 4" lengths to attach the head.

The dried apple head can be left as it is or painted, using liquid make-up or felt pens and string or wool hair added, pearl beads on pins can also be used to make eyes. The doll can be dressed in anything, in any way, a cloak of collected natural objects such as leaves, twigs, pips and peelings, or in fabric printed with apple prints.

If very large apples are used then these dolls can be made into puppets by taking out the core to about half way up, inserting a cylinder of stiff card and using like a glove puppet. The larger the apple, the longer it takes to dry out. Cooking apples would work best for these, such as Bramley or Howgate Wonder, however some go soft as they get older so it would be best to use them early in the season. Smaller dessert apples which are late keepers, but firm, like Ashmead's Kernel or Ribston Pippin would also be suitable. *Ryedale District Council, Yorks '92, Colne Valley Groundwork Trust, Middlesex '93 & Cider Museum, Hereford '93*

Apple Wreath or Kissing Bough

Glue dried apple rings on a flat cardboard ring, or using three strands of stiff wire, loosely plaited together and tie the rings on. Decorate with ribbons, greenery, cinnamon sticks and candles. Hang with apples.

Decorated apples

Apple clove balls were used in Elizabethan times and hung in closets. Use a firm apple such as a late keeping dessert like Ribston Pippin or Ashmead's Kernel and push cloves into the sides to form a pattern. Hang from a ribbon attached to the stalk. *The Brewhouse, Somerset '92*

'The Gift'

Apple Gifts were once given on New Year's Day and at other times of the year as an offering of good health and friendship in the year to come. Help to re-invent this tradition by giving an apple 'Gift' on Apple Day, October 21st.

Carefully wash and dry a firm, largish apple, such as Annie Elizabeth, a cooker used by the Victorians for dining table displays, or a large dessert apple like Cornish Gilliflower or Belle de Boskoop. Decorate the sides by dipping it in melted honey or glue and rolling in oats. Raisins or cracked wheat can be stuck on and cloves or corn pushed into the sides of the apple. The stalk was originally decorated with evergreen, thyme and box, which can be attached with pins. Lastly push three cocktail or lollipop sticks into the sides of the apple to form a tripod for it to stand on. Originally these gifts also had a stick in the side of the apple to act as a handle or they hung from ribbons. (See pages 83-6)

Apple Hedgehogs

There are stories of hedgehogs carrying apples impaled on their spines. Some say that they climbed trees then threw themselves onto the fruit below.[13]

To make an apple hedgehog take a round apple, a large dessert apple rather than a cooker, Suntan, Blenheim Orange or Laxton's Superb are good varieties. Make four legs using matchsticks, cocktail or lollipop sticks, add currants for eyes and a mouth. Prickles are made from halved cocktail sticks, adorned with raisins, cheese, marzipan apples or even crab apples. *Gartmore Primary School, Stirling '92*

Paper-making
Make paper using a paper pulp containing apple leaves or bark, which produces a yellow dye. Leaves, strips of peel and pips can be laid onto the pulp when it is ready to be pressed flat. The paper can be used as packaging for giving apples. *Bromham Mill, Bedford '91*

Apple Prints
Take apples of different sizes and shapes, cut them cross ways to reveal the magic star. Dip in paint or use an ink pad and press onto paper. Each variety has its own special print depending on its shape and size. Try many varieties to see the great range. The apples can be cut downwards and into slices to create different patterns, leaves can also be printed in the same way. Use the prints to make friezes, decorate hats, T-shirts, apple boxes, badges, jewellery, tree decorations, posters, collages and banners. *Grove Farm, Oxon '91*

The Guinness Book of Apples
Draw different varieties of apples, weigh and measure them, to see which variety is the heaviest and which is the fattest. Try out different substances to see what prevents an

apple from going brown once it has been cut open. *Alderman Pounder Infants, Notts '93*

Necklaces
String dried apple rings or crab apples together to make necklaces. *Stroud, Gloucestershire '93*

Mobiles
Using rods or twigs and twine suspend apple shapes or cut out prints to make a mobile, add maggots and leaves and create a tree by using a series of different length rods. Real apples, dried apple rings or stuffed fabric apples can also be hung, either on their own or mixed in with prints and shapes.

Apple Day Banners
Make a banner or flag to celebrate Apple Day, October 21st, by sewing felt or fabric apples or printing apples onto cloth. *Ryedale Museums, North Yorkshire, '93*

Dabbling
Plant pips in a pot remembering that a tree that has been raised from a pip will not be true to its parent, but a new variety for you to name. *Gartmore Primary, Stirling; Colnbrook Combined & Poyle County First Schools, Middlesex '93*

Planting
Plant an apple tree of a local variety, looking at its position, method of planting, care throughout the year. Make regular

visits to create a diary of the tree recording its development by photographing, drawing and writing about it. *Gartmore Primary School, Stirling '92*

Recipes

Celebrate Apple Day with different apple dishes such as apple pie, crumble, snow, charlotte, baked apples, toffee or chocolate apples. Savoury dishes are good too, like apple and fennel salad, celeriac and apple soup or pork chops with apples, which can all be found in The Apple Source Book.

Hold a best decorated apple pie competition. Decorate pies with cut out pastry shapes, of leaves or apples. *Halcyon Centre, Redditch, Hereford '93*

Toffee Apples

Use small ripe apples with no bruises or blemishes.

For 10-12 apples:

4oz/100g butter

8oz/225g black treacle

1lb/450g brown sugar

1 tbsp vinegar
10-12 small apples

Wash and wipe dry the apples. Push a wooden stick into each, downwards through the core.

Mix the toffee ingredients together and boil for 20 minutes. Dip the apples in and stand on a rack or oiled greaseproof paper to set.[14]

A non-alcoholic Wassail Cup

4 apples
1 orange
1 lemon
1 pint (1/2 litre) apple juice
1 teaspoon cinnamon
pinch of ginger powder
4 cloves
2 teaspoonsful honey
1 pint (1/2 litre) water
6 small apples for decoration

Peel and chop all the fruit, except the six small apples and remove the pips. Put the chopped fruit, juice, spices and honey into a pan and add the water. Bring to the boil. Add the remaining small apples. Simmer for five minutes. Leave to cool slightly and drink.

Every year without fail apple trees were wassailed with song, dance and toasts to thank them for their fruit and to ensure they gave a good harvest in the coming season. Make

wassail shakers from papier mache to wake the trees. Choose a wassail King and Queen to pour apple juice on the roots and hang toast cut into shapes or edible apple tokens from bird seed in the branches for birds, the guardians of the trees. *Pinhoe Church School, Devon '93*
(see pages 73-82)

BOARD GAMES

The Apple Tree Man and the Orchard Scrumpers
This game for two players is similar to Nine Mens Morris. The board can either be drawn out on paper and counters used, or for an apple sized version make a clay or wood board with hollows carved out, or the pressed carboard fruit packing. The Apple Tree Man has one counter, placed in the

middle hole or cross, while the Orchard Scrumper's counters fill each hole or cross around the edge of the board, as in the diagram. The Apple Tree Man may move his counter to any adjacent space in any direction and capture the Scrumper's counters by jumping over them, but at the same time making sure he is not hemmed in. The

Scrumper's counters may only move one space and one counter per turn and may not jump or capture. The Apple Tree Man wins by capturing so many of the Scrumper's counters that he cannot be blocked by them. The Scrumper wins if his counters manage to successfully block the Apple Tree Man so he can no longer move.

Red Apples, Green Apples

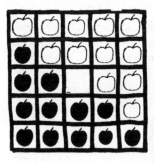

The board for the previous game can be used again for this one and again it is for two players. One has green apples or counters, while the other has red ones. They begin as in the diagram, and the object is to swap sides on the board. Counters can move in any direction, except backwards and jump over one another. The first to get all her counters to the other side in the original formation wins.

This board and layout can be used for apple solitaire which is played alone. The object is to be left with only one apple in the centre hole, the rest being removed when jumped over.

Branches and Ladders.

An apple version of snakes and ladders. Climb up the ladders and slide down on the broken branches whilst trying to collect as many apples as possible. On some squares apples are lost, while they are gained on others. The winner is the person with the most apples at the end of the game. Draw a tree against a brick wall, where every brick is a numbered square. The tree has some broken branches which span from one branch to another and ladders which lean up against the tree. The ladders are short cuts to a higher number, while players fall down the broken branches. Apples are scattered across the board to be collected, added dangers are squares with wasps on them to make players miss a go and dropped baskets so players have to start collecting apples all over again. The aim is to collect the most apples and to get to the end safely. *Sherford, Devon '93*

Adam and Eve

Draw a tree against a grid with ladders and snakes and a single apple near the top. Using a dice, as in Snakes and Ladders, take turns to move square by square, climbing the ladders and slipping down the snakes. First to the apple is Eve, after that you are on your own....

STORIES

In many cultures the apple was considered as the most mystical and supreme of all fruit. They are associated with many things: immorality; fruitfulness; offerings or distractions in suitor contests; cures; love charms; tests of chastity; means of fortune telling; magic objects; immortality. In Latin the apple was known as Pomona, after the goddess of fruit trees and was the general term used for all fruit.

The Isle of Avalon or the Apple Isle was the happy other world of Arthurian and Celtic legend, a magic island paradise of apple trees in the West. It was thought of as a wonderful place:

> Where falls not hail, nor rain, or any snow,
> Nor ever wind blows loudly, but it lies
> Deep-meadowed, happily, fair with orchard lawns,
> And bowery hollows crowned with summer sea.[15]

Heroes went to Avalon after death to wait for restoration and return to the mortal world. It was where King Arthur's sword was forged and where he was taken to be healed from his fatal wound. In Ireland Avalon was known as Emhaim Abhlach, where the hills were clothed with apple trees which bore both fruit and blossom at the same time.[16]

The apple tree was commonly grown by the early Britons, especially in Glastonbury in Somerset, which was known as

the 'Apple Orchard' because of the quantity of fruit grown there, prior to the Roman invasion. At one time Glastonbury was thought to have been Avalon, but some think this is due to an etymological error.[15]

Before the battle of Senlac, King Harold pitched his camp beside the 'hoar Apple tree', which was known as giving good luck to those about to go into battle.[15]

The Saxons highly prized the apple as shown in their Coronation Benediction:

May the Almighty bless thee with the blessings of heaven above, and the mountains and the valleys, with the blessings of the deep below, with the blessings of Grapes and Apples. Bless, O Lord, the courage of this Prince, and prosper the work of his hands; and by Thy blessing may this land be filled with Apples, with the fruit and dew of heaven, from the top of the ancient mountains, from the Apples of the eternal hills, from the fruits of the earth and its fullness.[15]

Saint Serf, on his way to Fife, threw his staff across the Firth of Forth, from Inch Keith to Culross, where it took root and became an apple tree known as Marglas.[15]

There is a West Highland tale about a hero who wanted to pass from Islay to Ireland. He pulled out sixteen apples, threw them into the sea, and stepped from one to another.[15]

A Gruacach, a hairy ogre,[17] had a golden apple, which he threw at anyone who came near him. If they didn't catch it they died. Eventually it was caught and thrown back where upon the Gruacach died.[15]

In Somerset it is believed by some that the AppleTree Man was the guardian of the orchard and lived in the oldest apple tree. Other spirits thought to be attached to the orchard were the Colt Pixy and Lazy Lawrence, the spirit of indolence.[12]

Isaac Newton - Laws of Gravity

Sir Isaac Newton, the renowned mathematician and thinker, was supposed to have discovered the laws of gravity in 1660 by seeing an apple fall from a tree in his garden at Woolsthorpe Manor between Grantham and Belvoir, Lincolnshire. The actual variety of tree was disputed and was originally thought to be a Flower of Kent. Now a descendant of the tree in Cambridge University Botanical Gardens is known as Isaac Newton's tree.[2]

In Greek and Roman mythology the apple tree which has

many legends about it, was dedicated to Aphrodite/Venus, who was often represented with the fruit in her hand.

Eurydice was carried off to fairyland because she slept under an apple tree.[15]

Golden apples are mentioned in many myths, however, they could have been pomegranates, oranges or apricots, but apples were more commonly known.[15]

The Garden of the Hesperides
The eleventh of Hercules' twelve labours was to take three golden apples from the Garden of the Hesperides. The garden, given to Juno by Jupiter as a wedding present was tended by three nymphs, the Hesperides, who turned trespassers to stone. The tree which bore these apples was in the middle of the garden, guarded by Ladon, a fierce dragon. Hercules managed to enter the garden

and steal the apples. However, on being removed the fruit tarnished, but on its return took on its former lustre.

Atlanta and Hippomenes - Atlanta's race

Atlanta, a very fast runner, announced she would only marry the man who could out race her, but if he lost then he would die. One by one men lost and died. However, Hippomenes, sought the help of Venus, who gave him three golden apples. Every time Atlanta gained on him he threw one a little ahead of her, as she paused to pick each up, he passed her. On the last occasion he crossed the finishing line ahead of her, so could marry her.[2]

Three Apples fell from Heaven

'Three apples fell from heaven', closes many Armenian and Turkish folktales, in a similar way to how we use ' and they lived happily ever after'. This phrase differs from place to place and probably from one storyteller to another.

Three apples fell from the sky, one for the teller of this story, another for the hearer of this story and a third for the child who might some day read it in a book! *Turkey*

There were three apples: one for me, one for the storyteller, and one for the listener, and the peel for the Sultan. This was often changed to: the peel for the mare, in case it sounded too disrespectful. *Iraq*

Three apples came from God, one for the teller, one for the one who asked for the tale and one for the one who gave his ear. *Armenia*

The use of this phrase could have come from the idea of giving apples as a sign of friendship or good will, but there is also a connection with the story of St Dorothea, who is represented holding three apples and three roses. Dorothea was persecuted for being a Christian and on her way to be executed she was taunted by one of the crowd to send some for the fruits from the heaven that she was about to enter. She stopped to pray before her death and an angel appeared with a basket of three apples and three roses. She sent these to the doubter in the crowd, who was so impressed he too was converted. Christianity later became the accepted religion of Armenia and to show they had converted to the new faith the closing of 'three apples fell from heaven or God...' was put into the stories.[18]

William Tell

At the time Switzerland was under the rule of Austria there was much unrest. William Tell, a good patriot, was reputed to be the best crossbowman in the country. His district was overseen by Gessler, a tyrant who decreed that

anyone who did not salute the Austrian Emblem would die. Tell refused and was immediately arrested. As part of his punishment his son was fetched, tied to a tree and an apple placed on his head. Tell was ordered to shoot the apple off his son's head. He took up his crossbow and two arrows. He shot the first one which split the apple in two and buried itself in the tree. He turned to Gessler and said: "If I'd hurt the boy the other arrow would have been in your heart." Instead of death Tell was condemned to prison, but while being taken across Lake Uri to the prison, a storm threatened to overturn the boat. Tell was also an excellent oarsman, therefore was untied and took control of the boat. As they approached the shore he escaped. Gessler threatened to kill the entire Tell family if William didn't give himself up. However Tell killed Gessler in an ambush before this happened. The Swiss inspired by his actions drove the Austrians out. William Tell was offered the crown of Switzerland, but he turned this down and returned to his life in the mountains.[2]

Johnny Appleseed

John Chapman from Leominster, Massachusetts, was a pioneer of apples and orchards in America and became known as Johnny Appleseed. He created the first apple nursery in Pennsylvania, gave saplings and seeds to families moving West, helped pioneers and settlers to grow and protect their orchards and travelled up and down the country planting apple trees in Ohio, Indiana, Illinois as well as

Pennsylvania. He was seen as a kind of living legend because of his peculiar ways, torn and ragged clothing, religious ecstasy, wild appearance and knowledge of woods and animals. He was never harmed by Indians who looked up to him as a saint and great medicine man. He died on 11th March 1847 from pneumonia following a journey to one of his orchards.[19]

The apple tree was the central tree of heaven in Iroquois Indian mythology. In a Wyandot myth, an apple tree shaded the lodge of the mighty ruler.[20]

SONGS AND RHYMES

St Paul's Steeple

Upon Paul's steeple stands a tree
As full of apples as may be
The little boys of London town
They run with hooks to pull them down;
And then they run from hedge to hedge
Until they come to London Bridge.

This is a very old rhyme popular before, both the current domed cathederal and 1561, when the steeple of the old St Paul's was destroyed by lightning.[2]

So Tommy did climb but the bough it did break (fall),
And down came poor Tommy with apples and all,
Apples and all, apples and all,
And down came poor Tommy with apples and all.
Forest of Dean,
Gloucestershire [21]

Common Ground

At Michaelmas and a little before,
Away goes the apple along with the core,
At Christmas and a little bit arter,
A crab in the hedge is worth looking arter!
Newbold on Avon, Warwickshire [22]

September blow soft,
Till the fruit's in the loft.[1]

A cherry year,
A merry year;
A pear year,
A dear year;
A plumb year,
A dumb year.[1]

Devon Horsemen's rhyme
Cider on beer, never fear.
Beer on cider, makes a bad rider.[9]

An apple pie without some cheese,
is like a kiss without a squeeze. *Yorkshire* [9]

Johnny Appleseed's Song
The Lord is good to me, and so I thank the Lord,
For giving me the things I need,
The sun, the rain and the apple seed,
The Lord is good to me.
Gartmore Primary School, Stirling

The Apple Alphabet

A was an apple pie
B bit it
C cut it
D dealt it
E ate it
F fought for it
G got it
H had it
I inspected it
J jumped for it
K kept it
L longed for it
M mourned for it
N nodded at it
O opened it
P peeped in it
Q quartered it
R ran for it
S stole it
T took it
U upset it
V viewed it
W wanted it
XYZ & ampersand
All wished for a piece in hand.[23]

Old Mother Eve

The apple tree stood in the garden
It's blossoms as white as the snow, the snow,
And there in the cool of the evening,
Our dear Lord God He did go, He did go.
But old Mother Eve she liked the apples,
And Adam he liked'en too, he liked'en too, he liked'en
too.

A serpent he hid in the garden
A-twined about the tree, the tree,
Yew never did eat of such wonderful meat
And so honey sweet! said he, he, he.
But old Mother Eve etc.

They turned 'em both out of the garden
Shut out with a fiery key, key, key,
But Old Man Adam rolled up his sleeves
And planted an apple-tree, tree, tree.
But old Mother Eve etc.

There are apple-trees down in the garden
There are orchets in the valley below, below
In autumn and spring the apple is King
And we bless it where ever we go, go, go.
For old Mother Eve etc.

Taunton, Devon [24]

A Wassailing song for Catterns Night, 25th November,
instead of Twelfth Night.

Poor Rodger is dead

Sir Rodger is dead and lies in his grave
Lies in his grave, lies in his grave,
Sir Rodger is dead and lies in his grave
Iar Ioh Ia

They planted an apple tree over his head
Over his head, over his head
They planted an apple tree over his head,
Iar Ioh Ia

There came an old woman a picking them up
A picking them up, a picking them up,
There came an old woman a picking them up,
Iar Ioh Ia

Old Rodger got up and gave her a knock
Gave her a knock, gave her a knock
Old Rodger got up and gave her a knock,
Iar Ioh Ia

Which made the old woman go hipperty hop
Go hipperty hop, go hipperty hop,
Which made the old woman go hipperty hop,
Iar Ioh Ia.[25]

Gather the apples, October man,
And the autumn leaves need clearing,
The days are short, the nights are long,
And Hallowe'en is nearing.[26]

There was a man, he went mad
He jumped into a paper bag;
The paper bag was too narrow,
He jumped into a wheelbarrow;
The wheelbarrow took on fire,
He jumped into a cow byre;
The cow byre was too nasty,
He jumped into an apple pasty;
The apple pasty was too sweet,
He jumped into Chester-le-Street;
Chester-le-Street was full of stones,
He fell down and broke his bones.[23]

Ride a cock-horse
To Banbury Cross,
To see what Tommy can buy;
A penny white loaf,
A penny white cake,
And a two-penny apple pie.[23]

APPLE SAYINGS

An apple a day, keeps the doctor away. **Eat an apple before going to bed, And make the doctor beg for his bread.**[27] Apples and pears - cockney rhyming slang for stairs. **Apples and rice or spice - nice, usually follows 'o very...', and means the opposite.** Apple fritter - bitter, as in beer. **Apple pie - sky.** Apple pips - lips.[28] **To upset the apple cart - to spoil a plan or intention, originally the apple cart stood for the human body.**[29] The Apple - the earth or globe.[10] **Apple Pie order - everything neat and correct.**[30] Apple cheeks/Apple faced - to have rosy cheeks or to blush.[29] **A goodly apple, rotten at the heart - someone who appears to be good, but is bad underneath,** *Shakespeare's 'The Merchant of Venice'.*[31] An apple may be fair without and bad within.[32] **Mani appel is uten grene, briht on beme (tree) and biter with-innen,** *Proverbs of Alfred.*

Appeles and peres that semen very goode, Full ofte tyme are roten by the core. **Even red apples are wormy,** *Germany.* Apple of one's eye - something precious, originally meant the pupil of the eye, which was thought to be a solid ball like an apple. **The apple of discord - anything that causes trouble, from the myth connected to the Trojan wars.**[29] A Costermonger - someone who sold Costard apples, but came to mean anyone who sold fruit. **An Apple-wife or Apple-woman - a woman who sells apples.** A windfall - unexpected good fortune, usually a legacy.[10] **Of a wavering and fickle mind; as we say with children, won with an apple and lost with a nut.**[21] The fairest apple hangs on the highest bough, *Scotland.*[29] **Apples are sweet, when they are plucked in the garden-er's absence.** Stolen apples are the sweetest.[33] **The apples on the other side of the wall are sweet-est.** Reach for the highest apples first; you can get the low ones any time.[29] **Who sets an apple tree may live to see its end. Who sets a pear may set it for a friend.**[34] The apple never falls far from the tree - continuity of family traits, usually bad ones.[33]

Not worth the paring of a rotten apple.[30] Not worth a rotten apple.[32] **There's small choice in rotten apples.**[21] The rotten apple injures its neighbours. **A rotten apple spoils its companions.** One bad apple can spoil the whole barrel.[33] **A rotted apple among the whole maketh rottie those around.**[21] An apple, an egg and a nut, you may eat though dressed as a slut. **As like an apple to an oyster - two things that are totally different.** Every hog own his apple.[30] **Comfort me with apples: for I am sick of love,** *Song of Solomon.*[29] Better an apple given than eaten - taking what is paltry or bad.[30] **An apple is better given than eaten by time,** *Scotland.*[29] No good apples on sour stock.[30] **There is an art even in roasting apples,** *Germany.* To the immature, all apples are green, *Marian Randolph, 'Grim grow the lilacs',.*

As round as an apple. As sweet as apples. **The more apples the tree bears the more the tree bows.** To spare neither the apple nor the colk (core) - To do all one can.[32] **The crab of the wood is sauce very good for the crab of the sea, But the wood of the crab is sauce for a drab that will not her husband obey.**[35] He that will not a wife wed, Must eat a cold apple when he goeth to bed - apples were supposed to have a similar effect to cold baths. **Where the apples reddens, never pry Lest we lose our Eden, Eve and I.** *Robert Browning, 'A woman's last word'.*[29] Sodom apples, outwardly fair, ashes at the core.[30] **To give an apple where there is an orchard - selfishness in giving.**[35] Those who have an orchard shall have an apple lent to them. And those who have a horse shall have another sent them. *Shropshire.* **Plant the crab where you will, it will never bear pippins - don't expect good results from unreasonable causes.** As sure as God made little apples on big trees[29] or As sure as God made little green apples - to be absolutely certain or sure.[36] **Applesauce - rubbish or waffle, 'I wasn't born yesterday. I know apple sauce when I hear it.'**[29] An Apple-jack in East Anglia is an apple turnover, whereas in America it is a drink similar to Calvados.[17] **In America an apple can have many meanings: a ball in baseball; a person when preceeded by an adjective, He's a slick apple; a lively street, district, large town or city, which came from the 1930's jazz musicians; a native American who has taken on the values and behaviour of the white community.** An Applejack cap - a round, knitted, brightly coloured cap with a wide brim and a pom-pom, mainly worn by African Americans, *America*.[36] **As American as Apple pie,** *America*.[10] The Big Apple or The Apple - New York City, there was also a jitterbug dance in the late 1930's of the same name, *America*. **An apple for the teacher.** To Apple polish or Apple butter - to flatter in order to get personal gain, originally connected to the highly polished apples pupils gave to their teachers. Someone who does this is known as an Apple polisher, *America*. A wise apple - a know-all or smart alec, *America*.[36] **A smart apple - an intelligent or wise person, 'he's one smart apple',** *America*. A sad apple - an obnoxious or pessimistic person, *America*.[37] **An apple head - An idiot,** *America*.[36] An apple-knocker - a migratory fruit picker, or unsophisticated country per-son. The name comes from the practise of knocking ap-ples out of trees, *America*.[28] **Apple pies - eyes,** *America*. Apple and banana - piano, *America*. **Apple-pie-and-motherhood - having obvi-ous and unexceptional vir-tues. 'They'll always vote yes on an apple-pie-and-motherhood issue,'** *America*. A ground apple - a rock, used by lumberjacks, *America*. **Ally apple, Road apple or Horse apple -**

horse manure, *America*. An hen apple - an egg, *America*.

To swallow the apple - to become tense and ineffective, a term used by sportsmen, *America*. How do you like them apples! - exclamation of pleasure and triumph, *America*.[36] The first recorded written use of the apple in English was by King Alfred, around 885. He used the words Redan Apla - red apple in his English translation of Pope Gregory I's Pastoral Care.[21]

PART II

SEASONAL CUSTOMS AND BELIEFS

AUTUMN

Michaelmas Day, September 29th, was the time for Apple Grabbing when crab apples were gathered to be stored until old Michaelmas Day, October 11th.[12]

Apple Day, October 21st, is an annual celebration of the diversity of apples and other tree fruit which can be grown in this country. Initiated by Common Ground in 1990, it is now celebrated in hundreds of places and by thousands of people across the country.

Hallowe'en, 31st October, All Saints' or All Hallow's Day, 1st November and All Souls' Day, 2nd November, were dedicated to thoughts of the dead and associated with Samhain, the Celtic feast of the Dead. Children and the very poor went Souling, singing at houses and asking for something in return, which at this time of year was often apples. Originally special cakes were baked,  but later anything that was given was called a soul cake. Souling songs, were different to many other begging songs in that they not only offered good will to the master and mistress of the house, but also to their servants and live-stock. Souling was mainly practised in Cheshire, Stafford-shire, Shropshire, Derbyshire and Lancashire, the custom was the same in all these counties, but each had its own particular songs and names for this custom.

In Cheshire the custom was known as 'Soul-caking', and participants often dressed up in elaborate costumes with blackened faces, and a hobby-horse and sometimes a play was performed.

> Soul, soul for an apple or two,
> If you've no apples, pears will do;
> If you've no pears, a good jug of beer
> Will last us all till this time next year.[8]

Souling night has come at last,
And we are souling here;
And all that we are souling for
Is apples and good cheer.[8]

A traditional song from Staffordshire:
Soul day! Soul!
The roads are very dirty,
Our shoes are very thin;
Pray good missis and master,
Pop a penny in.
An apple, a pear, a plum, or a cherry,
Or any good thing to make us merry
If you haven't an apple, a pear will do,
If you haven't a pear, good money will do,
One for Peter, two for Paul,
Three for them as made us all.
Soul day! Soul!
The cock sat up in the yew tree,
The hen came cackling by,
We wish you a merry Christmas,
And a fat pig in the sty.
Soul day! Soul![8]

Souling songs varied in length and content, depending on the area, however towards the end of the 19th century as the custom began to die out, they grew shorter as verses were forgotten or not recorded and only the most memorable snippets used. The following one from North Staffordshire recorded in 1954 illustrates this well.

Soul, Soul for an apple or two
If you've got no apples, pears will do;
If you've got no pears, ha'pennies will do,
If you've got no ha'pennies, God Bless You.[3]

In Shropshire, Souling, which took place on Hallowe'en or All Saints' night was known as 'Whistle Wassail' night.

Whistle, wassail,
Bread and possel,
An apple or a pear,
A plum or a cherry,
Any good thing to make us merry.
One for Peter, one for Paul,
Three for the man who made us all.
So up with the kettle and down with the pan,
Give us an answer and we'll begone.[8]

Wissel a wassle about
Give us some red apples to throw them all down
One for Peter and one for Paul
And one for little Jack up in the hall
Holly and ivy, mistletoe
Give us a red apple and let us go.[38]

In Ireland Hallowe'en was celebrated with special dishes such as Apple Amber, Apple Dumplings, which had money in them, and Friars' Omelette or Apple Fritters.[39]

In the Forest of Dean, Gloucestershire, on Bonfire Night, 5th November, boys went from house to house demanding

cider or a ha'pence. If refused they would lift the garden gate
off its hinges.[21]

On St Clement's Day, 23rd November, blacksmiths went
Clemening, visiting each house and singing in return for
apples and beer. It was practised originally by blacksmiths,

since St Clement
was their patron
saint, but later by
children. In North
Warwickshire
this was known as
'Clementsing'
and in Leicester-
shire as 'Going a
Gooding'.   St
Clement was said
to be the son of St
Catherine, patron saint of spinners, whose feast falls on 25th
November, therefore her name is sometimes mentioned in
Clemening rhymes. Apple bobbing was also played on this
day so it was sometimes known as Bite Apple Day.[40]

Clemany! Clemany! Clemany! Mine!
A good red apple and a pint of wine!
Staffordshire [41]

Cattern and Clemen be here, here, here,
Give us your apples and give us your beer!
Sussex[41]

Many of the songs for these Autumn and Winter feast days
followed a similar pattern. However each differed just
slightly enough to make it special to the area.

Cattern and Clemen come year by year,
Give us your apples and give us your beer,
Some for Peter, some for Paul,
Some for the merry boys under your wall,
Peter was a good man,
For his sake give us some;
None of the worst, but some of the best,
And pray God send your souls to rest.
Butler, Butler fill the bowl,
Dash it up against the wall;
Up the ladder and down the can,
Give us a red apple and we'll be gone.
A plum, a plum, a cherry, a cherry,
A cup of perry will soon make us all merry.
We go a cattin, a cattin we go,
From Hitton to Tritton, as soon as you shall see;
From Hitton to Pitton, Hartlebury all three,
Round by old Kiddy, and good Hillintree,
Then down to old Arley, Astley and Strawley go nimbly,
And finish up at Holt, Hallow and Grimley.
Herefordshire[34]

St Clement's, St Clement's, St Clement's is here,
Apples and pears are very good cheer!
One for St Peter, one for St Paul
And three for him who made us all.
Up with the kettle and down with the pan,
Give us some apples and we'll begone.
Market Bosworth, Leicestershire [8]

Over sixty children of the Church of England School, Enville, celebrated the feast of St Clement in traditional manner. The feast, which symbolises the gathering of the apple crop, was revived by Miss M. E. Steward (Headmistress) in 1961. The sixty-eight children marched to Enville Hall, where they sang their Clemeny song, then each received an apple. The butler at the Hall, Mr A. A. Longbottom, then showered the children with hot pennies from a shovel. *Stourbridge County Express, November 27th 1965*[42]

On St Clement's Day apples and nuts were thrown from the windows of the Guildhall in Walsall, West Midlands. This custom was abolished in 1860.[8]

St Catherine was the Patron Saint of Wheel Wrights, Spinners and Lacemakers and also protector of unmarried women. On St Catherine's Eve, 24th November, in Worcestershire lace makers prepared a special drink. Apples were roasted in front of an open fire until their pulp fell into a bowl of cider spiced with sugar and cinnamon set beneath. When all the apple pulp was caught and mixed, it was strained and offered to guests in the 'Cathern Bowl'.[8] The apple paring custom associated with Hallowe'en and other divination games were also practised on this night.[40]

In Worcestershire Catterning was also practised a month later on St Thomas' Day, 21st December.[21]

WINTER

The Kissing Bough was the traditional Christmas decoration in Britain, prior to 1840, when the Christmas tree was introduced by Prince Albert. A garland of greenery and mistletoe was hung with red apples and candles,[41] which were lit every night from Christmas Eve through until Twelfth Night.[39]

On Christmas Eve at Peniston, South Yorkshire, a large apple pie would be made. The whole family sat round the kitchen table and the pie was passed round, each member eating some in turn using the same spoon. A jar of posset, ale mixed with milk, was also passed round and drunk from the spoon in the same manner.[8]

Apple pies were once served as a Christmas pudding, such as Bedfordshire Apple Florentine.[14]

The sun shining through the apple trees on Christmas

morning (or in some districts, Easter morning) was a sign of a good crop and a prosperous year for the owner of the orchard.[43]

Worsting, Howling or Youling was a ceremony similar to wassailing, practised in Western and Southern counties as well as parts of Wales on Christmas morning. Participants known as Howlers were led by a trumpeter with a ram's horn to the orchard where the trees were rapped with clubs to the accompaniment of the horn, to frighten away any evil spirits, and wake the sleeping tree sprits. The procession then was led to the farmer's house, or local pub, where, having sung for admission, the Howlers were feted with ale.[8]

At Hastings, Sussex, on New Year's Day, tradesmen threw out their surplus stocks of apples left over from Christmas, to be scrambled for by the fishermen and boys, who went to the shops and encouraged this by shouting: Throw out! Turn out![8]

In Worcestershire on St. Valentine's Day, 14th February, children went from house to house asking for apples, which they saved to make apple fritters on Shrove Tuesday.[8]

On Collop Monday and Shrove Tuesday boys went from door to door, knocking with clubs, accompanied by rhymes begging for apples, pancakes or dumplings:

Shrovetide is nigh at hand
And we are come a-shroving.
Pray, dame, give something,
An apple or a dumpling.[3]

In parts of the country this also took place on Fritter or Ash
Wednesday. There is a reference to this custom in some
versions of the rhyme Oranges and Lemons:

'Pancakes and Fritters', say the bells of St. Peter's,
'Two sticks and an apple', say the bells of Whitechapel.[1]

SPRING

Blessing the apple trees with a Youling Ceremony, similar
also to Wassailing, took place at Ascensiontide in Kent.
Young men rushed round the orchards, encircling trees and
chanting:

Standfast root; bear well top;
God send us a youpling sop
Every twig apple big,
Every bough apple enow![8]

If they weren't rewarded afterwards with ale they cursed the
trees and their owners. The same ceremony took place at
West Wickham, Buckinghamshire, during Rogation Week,
the fifth Sunday after Easter.[15]

Contradictions are commonplace between different versions of similar beliefs.

March dust on the apple leaf
Brings all kind of fruit to grief.[21]

If the apple trees bloom in March
For barrels of cider you need not search
If the apple trees bloom in May
You can eat apple dumplings every day.[21]

When apple trees are in blossom in April and before May
You can put your barrels away.
But if they blossom at the end of May and at the beginning of June,
You can get your barrels in tune.[21]

On May 19th, St Dunstan's Day, great care was taken with the apple trees and the Saint was blamed if the new buds were nipped by a late frost. St Dunstan made beer and was supposed to have sold himself to the devil in return for the apple trees being blighted to stop any cider being produced.[15]

SUMMER

On Midsummer's Eve fires were lit under trees in orchards in Hertfordshire and Somerset to bless the apples. This also took place on St James' Day, 25th July, when priests would bless the apples.[15]

In Herefordshire it was believed that unless the orchards were christened with rain on St Peter's Day, June 29th, the crop would not be good.[21]

St Swithin's Day, 15th July, was also thought of as apple christening day.[30] Apples were supposed to be unfit for food until after this day, when they were blessed with a shower of rain.[34]

> Till St Swithin's Day be past
> The apples be not fit to taste![9]

In parts of Kent and Surrey people would gather in the orchards for this custom. It was thought that all the apples found on the trees on this day would mature and ripen.[8]

An Apple Pie Fair has been held in Marldon, Devon on August 25th since 1888 in memory of a local farmer, George Hill. Every year he gave windfalls to his workers to make an enormous apple pie for the village. Nowadays lots of small pies are made and hidden under a big crust and an Apple-pie Princess is crowned.[41]

On the Sunday after Holy-Rood or Holy-Cross Day, 14th September, at Avening, Gloucestershire, a pig's head and apple dumplings were taken to the bell ringers up in the church tower. This was known locally as Pig Face Sunday.[8]

The Cumberland Crab Fair in Egremont has been held on the nearest Saturday to September 18th, since 1267. Originally the lord of the manor distributed money to the crowd as he rode round the fair, but crab apples have taken the place of this and are scrabbled for.[5]

At Norton, nr Yeovil, Somerset, on the Sunday after the Nativity of the Virgin Mary, 19th September, the feast day in the old calendar, families would gather together and celebrate with apple pie.[8]

WASSAILING

'Wassail' comes from the Anglo Saxon 'wes hal', 'was haile' or 'wase hail' to be in good health or be fortunate.

WASSAILING THE APPLE ORCHARDS

Wassailing apple orchards traditionally took place between Christmas and 18th January, Twelfth Night in the old calendar. The idea was to protect the trees from evil spirits and to make sure they bore a plentiful fruit crop in the

coming season. The best or oldest tree in the orchard was chosen to represent them all, it was known as the Apple Tree Man, and was feted as a guardian of the orchard. [12] Cider was poured on the roots, pieces of toast or cake soaked in cider were laid in its fork or hung from the branches for the robins who were also considered the guardian spirits of the trees. The tips of the lowest branches were drawn down and dipped into the cider pail and the tree was toasted with cider and songs. Then the trees were rapped and sometimes the bark was torn. A huge din was made to drive away any evil spirits and wake the sleeping trees, trays and buckets were beaten, cow or ram horns blown and latterly shot guns fired through the top-most branches. The practical explanation for this was that all the commotion dislodged insects from the bark and the tearing was supposed to bring fruit earlier. Many believed that if the trees weren't wassailed then there would be no apples.

Although many similarities can be perceived in the ceremonies and songs they all differed from place to place across the country, where each created its own special way of celebrating its orchards.

Here's to thee, old apple tree
Whence thou may'st bud and whence thou may'st blow,
And whence thou may'st bear apples enow.
Hats full, Caps full, Bushel, Bushel sacks full,
And my pockets full too!
Huzza! [41]

In Sussex this custom was known as 'Worsling'.[15] Here and in parts of Devon parties of boys visited the orchards on New Year's Day, where they encircled the apple trees and chanted:

> Stand fast, bear well top,
> Pray God send us a howling crop;
> Every twig, apples big;
> Every bough, apples enow,
> Hats full, caps full,
> Full quarter sacks full.[8]

This was followed by a great shout and the trees were rapped with sticks.

In some orchards the men showed the trees what was required of them by bowing down to the ground three times and rising up slowly, miming the actions of lifting a heavy sack of apples.[44]

> Yer's tu thee, old apple-tree,
> Be zure yu bud, be zure yu blow
> And bring voth apples gude enough.
> Hats vul! Caps vul!
> Dree bushel-bags vul!
> Pockets vul and awl!
> Urrah! Urrah!
> Aw'ess, hats vul, caps vul.
> And dree bushel-bags vul.
> Urrah! Urrah!
> *Devon* [8]

In pre-Christian times Aeolus, the God of the Winds, was called upon to blow a gale because it was thought that high winds were good for the trees as they moved the roots, so they would bear a better crop.

A song from Upton St. Leonards, Gloucestershire, reflects this:

> Blowe, blowe, bear well,
> Spring well in April,
> Every sprig and every spray
> Bear a bushel of apples against
> Next New Year's Day.[45]

Part of the ceremony in Devon orchards involved lifting a small boy up on to one of the branches where he sat crying: "Tit, tit, more to eat", and was fed with bread, cheese and cider. He represented a tom tit or some type of small bird, who was thought to be the guardian spirit of the trees. It was hoped that with this performance the trees would be looked after in the coming year. There is an interesting parallel with a Japanese custom where the tree was threatened as opposed to being appeased in order to get a harvest. Two men visited the trees on New Year's Eve, one climbed the tree while the other stood at the bottom with an axe. He would ask the tree if it would bear well in the coming year and warn it that if it didn't then it would be cut down. The man in the tree replied as the spirit of the tree: "I will bear well".[8]

A song from Norton Fitzwarren, Nr Taunton, Somerset:

Old Apple-tree, we wassail thee,
And hoping thou wilt bear
For the Lord doth know where we shall be
Til apples come another year;
For us to bear well and to bloom well,
So merry let us be,
Let every man take off his hat
And shout to the old Apple-tree;
Old Apple-tree, we wassail thee,
And hoping thou wilt bear
Hats-fulls, caps-fulls,
Three bushel bag-fulls,
And a little heap under the stair.[46]

At Roadwater in Somerset, the wassailers returned to the local inn after the ceremony at the orchard. They entered by the back door, drank to the health of the house, and left by the front. This was never reversed, or else it would have brought bad luck to the house and probably the orchard as well.[43]

At Bridgwater in Somerset wassailing took place on 17th January in the evening, with a song handed down from father to son:

> Wassail, wassail, all around the town,
> The zider cup is white, and the zider is brown.[8]

In Cornwall the 'Warzale' was a toasting cry. In Warleggan on Christmas Eve trees were wassailed with cider, gun fire and singing and a small bough from the tree was placed in a bottle as part of the ceremony.[8]

At Camberley in Surrey the song began in a low mumble which gradually grew louder and louder:

> Here stands a good old apple tree.
> Stand fast root,
> Every bough apples enow,
> Every twig apples big.
> Hats-fulls, cap-fulls,
> Four and twenty sack-fulls.
> Hip, hip, hurrah! [8]

Old apple tree we'll wassail thee and hoping thou wilt bear
The lord does know where we shall be to be merry another
year
To blow well and bear well so merry let us be
Let every man drink up his cup and health to the old apple tree
Apples now hatfuls, capfuls, three bushel bagsfuls,
tallets 'olefuls, barns floorfuls, little heap under the stairs
Hip, hip, hip hooray.[21]

In Carhampton, Somerset and a few other places the ceremony has continued. It is undergoing a revival now in North Devon, Norton Fitzwarren, Somerset, Much Marcle, Herefordshire, and other places where the orchards are wassailed on the nearest Saturday to Twelfth Night. Wassailing also takes place in apple growing regions round Yakima, Washington, America. It was supposed to have been introduced by someone who had visited the ceremony at Carhampton in Somerset.[9]

THE WASSAIL BOWL

As well as wassailing apple orchards there was also a custom of taking the wassail bowl round from house to house. This traditionally took place after dark during the Twelve Days of Christmas and often in the last weeks of Advent too. The Wassail brew was a mixture of hot ale, spices, sugar and roasted apples, sometimes with eggs and thick cream floating on it, known as Lamb's Wool in

Gloucestershire, and was also drunk on St Catherine's Day, 25th November. The bowl was traditionally made from apple wood, often elaborately carved and kept for this purpose only. Wassailers carried bunches of evergreens hung with apples, oranges and coloured ribbons and sung

for entry at each house, where they collected alms in return for good luck wishes for the New Year and some of the brew.

A traditional New Year Wassail song:

> Our Wassail we do fill
> With apples and with spice
> Then grant us your goodwill
> To taste here once or twice
> Of our good Wassail.

A carol from Truro, Cornwall celebrating the apple tree:

> Now, Christmas is over, our Wassail begin
> Pray open your doors and let us come in.
>
> Good Mistress and Master sitting down by the fire,
> While we poor Wassail boys are trav'lin' the mire.
>
> I hope that your apple trees will prosper and bear,
> And bring forth good cider when we come next year.
>
> And we poor Wassail boys a'growin' weary and old,
> Drop a small piece of silver into our bowl.
>
> We're here in this place, we want you t'und'stand
> We're the jolly Wassail boys with a bowl in our hand.
>
> Good Mistress and Master, how can you forbear,
> Come fill up our bowl with cider or beer.

I hope you've had a merry Christmas, and we wish you a
Happy New Year,
With plenty of money and plenty of good cheer.

I wish you a blessing and a long time to live,
Since you've been so free and so willing to give.
Chorus:
To our Wassail,
Wassail, Wassail, Wassail,
And joy come to our jolly Wassail.[46]

Not far away in Portreath, Cornwall 'The Warzail' sounds
very different:
Misses and master sitting down by the fire
Put 'ee hand in thee pocket and give what 'zire
Warzail, Warzail, Warzail, Warzail
Let joy come down to your jolly warzail.

I hope your oxen may feed very fair
That you will have beef and some to spare
Warzail etc.

Where you got apples; hope you'll have ten
That you may have cider when we come again
Warzail etc.[38]

The tunes to these songs are also particular to the places, in
some of the references the music can be found.

APPLE GIFTING

Gifting took place on different days throughout the year in apple growing counties and some parts of Wales. Decorated apples were taken from house to house as a sign of friendship, good health and were supposed to bring good luck. They symbolised sweetness, fertility and immortality. In Christian symbolism these were associated with the offerings of the Three Wise Men, but are also thought to be connected to the Druids.

'The Gift' was an apple smeared with flour or meal and stuck with oats, wheat grains, corn or raisins. Three sticks were pushed into it for it to stand on, with a skewer inserted in one side as a handle, so it could be held without touching the sides. The top was trimmed with sprigs of box, yew, thyme or some kind of sweet smelling evergreen, which was often hung with nuts, especially hazels, since they could be attached to the ends of the leaves as the shells would clasp the foliage. The apples were finally

powdered with wheaten flour and parts touched up with gold leaf.[8]

In Glamorganshire apple gifts known as the Calennig were taken round from early on New Year's Day until noon.
New Year is marked by all the children in the neighbourhood forming themselves into little groups and carrying from house to house their congratulations and good wishes for health and prosperity during the ensuing year, which are symbolized by each bearing in his hand an apple stuck full of corn, variously coloured and decorated with a sprig of some evergreen, three short skewers serve as supports to the apple when not held in the hand, and a fourth serves to hold it by, without destroying its many coloured honours. *West Glamorgan* [47]

In Worcestershire at Castle Marton and Longdon until the 1950's, children visited farmhouses early on New Year's morning, where they sang the following song without taking a breath:

> Bud well, bear well, God send you fare well;
> Every sprig and every spray
> A bushel of apples next New Year's day.
> A happy New Year
> A pocket full of money
> A cellar full of beer.
> Please give me a New Year's gift.[8]

In Herefordshire a small pyramid made of leaves, apples, nuts was taken from house to house. Turnips as well as apples were also decorated with oats and flowered and given as a 'gilt'.[39]

Apples were given at other times throughout the year. One such time was St Thomas's Day, 21st December:

> Bud well, bear well
> God send fare well,
> A bushel of apples to give
> On St Thomas's morning.[34]

Up until 1890 on the Saturday nearest to Hallowe'en in Penzance, Cornwall, greengrocers laid in stocks of very large apples, locally known as Allan apples. These were given to each member of the family to be eaten on Hallowe'en, for luck. Older girls put them under their pillows before eating them to dream of their sweethearts.[8]

Apples were presented at Ripon Collegiate Church, Yorkshire on Christmas Day. Singing (choir) boys brought large baskets of red apples, each decorated with a sprig of rosemary, into the church to give to members of the congregation in return for money.[8]

In Worcestershire Apple Gifts were offered during the Catherning season, 23-25th November.[8]

Traditions have to begin somewhere, and at some time. In 1994 Gifting for Apple Day, October 21st, was initiated by

Common Ground building upon the traditions described. From giving special gift packs of mixed or single varieties of British grown traditional apples to a single apple with a ribbon tied round it, it is hoped that Gifting on Apple Day will become second nature, like giving eggs at Easter and cards at Christmas.

APPLE THROWING

In Kidderminster, Worcestershire, the Mayoral Elections took place on Michaelmas Day, 29th September when the new bailiff of the town was elected. From about 3-4 in the afternoon 'Kellums'[41] or the lawless hour took place. This was the time between the retirement of one bailiff and the beginning of his successor, when locals threw cabbage stalks at one another and no one could be arrested for damage to property or personal injury. At 4pm the bailiff elect and corporation made their way to the town house, when people would gather along the route to throw apples at the procession.[8]

At Clent in Worcestershire 'Crabbing the Parson' took place on the first Sunday after St Kenelm's Day, 17th July. All villagers and anyone else who chose armed themselves with crab apples. As the parson approached the church he was pelted with crabs

till he reached the porch. The use of sticks and stones instead of apples led to the suppression of this custom.[8] Crab or Kenelm's Wake, is also recorded as taking place on the first Sunday after 28th July, but was abolished at the beginning of the 19th Century.[41]

Revel Sunday at Hawkridge, Somerset, took place on the nearest Sunday to St. Giles' Day, 1st September, when the rector was pelted with apples on his way from the Rectory to the church.[8]

Crabbing the Parson at Mobberley, Cheshire took place on the following Sunday after St Luke's Day, 18th October.[8]

After the evening service on Easter Sunday at Northmore, nr Witney, Oxfordshire, apples were thrown in the church-yard. Those that had been married that year had to throw three times as many as anyone else. Afterwards the congregation went to the vicarage for bread, cheese and ale. The vicar was under obligation to provide the best cheese he could get.[8]

DIVINATIONS

Foretelling the future using apples was most often practised at Hallowe'en. All parts of the apple, from the pips to the peel, were used.

BY PIP

Apple pips were supposed tell whether or not a girl's lover or suitor was true and if their union would be happy.
An apple pip named after a lover was placed on the bars of the fire while this charm was recited:

>   If you love me, bounce and fly,
>   If you hate me, lie and die.[1]

If the pip spurted it meant the lover was true, if it burnt away he was false.

However in Sussex the opposite was true. The silent burning of two pips foretold a smooth courtship with a happy ending, whilst a bursting pip foretold the break up of the affair.[43]

In Lancashire prospective partners each placed a pip on a pair of tongs, left side for the woman, right side for the man. The tongs were placed in a hollow part of the fire and if both pips flew off on the same side, the pair would marry; if on opposite sides they wouldn't; and if both burnt together without flying off, the man would never propose. [48]

If a girl had more than one suitor rivalry between them could be transferred to the apple pips. She could name each pip and stick one on each cheek (or forehead of there were more than two). The last to fall was the one that loved her truly. [5]

If a person wanted to discover the direction in which their future partner lived, the pips were consulted. In Lancashire this practice involved moving in a circle, whilst holding an apple pip between the finger and thumb, which when squeezed flew in the supposed direction of the lover's residence. At the same time they would repeat:

> Pippin, pippin, paradise,
> Tell me where my true love lies:
> East, west, north or south,
> Pulling Brig or Cocker-mouth. [48]

A similar Welsh custom to this one was to hold an apple pip in the left hand and cover it with the right, whilst shaking both hands up and down and repeating:

> Kernel, kernel of the apple tree,
> Tell me where my true love be,
> East, west, north or south?
> Pretty kernel, tell the truth.

The kernel was examined and whichever way the pointed end was found was the direction from which the true love would come. [48]

In the Channel Isles on St John's Eve, 23rd June, couples took an apple and cut it in two. If the pips on each half were equal in number, the two would be married shortly; if the halves contained an unequal number of pips the one who held the half with the most would marry first. If a pip were cut in two, it denoted trouble to the one holding the larger portion. If two pips were cut, it meant early death or widowhood to one of the pair. The flavour of the apple, sour or sweet indicated the temper of the pair.[49]

BY PULP

Eating an apple at Hallowe'en was thought to reveal the identity of a person's future partner.

In Scotland it was thought that if a girl looked into a mirror lit by a single candle whilst eating an apple, she would see the the face of whom she would marry looking over her shoulder. Some versions of this

tradition say that she should comb her hair at the same time.[5]

In Murinigatt, Kirkcudbright, Galloway, the performer took an apple in one hand, a lighted candle in the other, placed herself in front of a mirror and ate the apple in the name of 'Uncle Geordie' - the devil. The face of her future husband appeared in the mirror when the last mouthful was eaten. The fear was that the face in the mirror would be that of 'Uncle Geordie'.[7]

Sometimes the apple was cut into nine pieces, eight of which would by eaten by the inquirer, while the ninth was held on a knife or fork or thrown over the left shoulder to be taken by their future husband or wife.[7]

Single young people each fastened an apple to a string and twirled it round in front of a fire. The one whose apple fell off first would be the first to marry; the one which remained till last belonged to the person who would die unwed.

In Devon, before Michaelmas, girls would gather crab apples, take them to a loft and arrange them in the form of their lovers' initials. Those found in the best condition on Michaelmas Day, 29th September, indicated the couple most likely to marry.[5]

To discover the initials of the person she would marry a girl twisted the stalk of an apple whilst reciting the alphabet, a letter for each twist. The letter she reached when the stalk came off was the initial of the first name of the man she would marry. To find that of his second name, she tapped the apple with the stalk, again reciting the alphabet until the stalk pierced through the skin.[41]

On Hallowe'en night an apple placed under the pillow would bring dreams of who a girl would marry.[43]

If a girl slept with an apple under her pillow on St Andrew's night, 30th November or Christmas night, and took it to the next festival of the church, the first man she saw, other than a relative, would become her husband.[8]

On St Thomas's Eve, 20th December, in Guernsey and other parts of the Channel Isles, a girl could discover the identity of her future husband by passing two new pins crosswise through a Golden Pippin apple (it had to be that variety) or nine in the eye

and nine in the tail of the apple, wrapping it in the stocking
or garter taken from her left leg, and placing it on her pillow.
She got into bed backwards, whilst reciting a long incanta-
tion to St. Thomas three times, then did not speak another
word. If the ceremony had been performed correctly she
would dream of her future husband.[49]

BY PEEL

The apple peeling or paring was often used to discover the
initial or name of a future partner.

The Feast of St Simon and St Jude, October 28th, was
thought to be a day especially lucky for divination. The
person who wished to see the identity of their future
partner peeled an apple in one strip, then standing holding
the peeling in their right hand repeated:

> St Simon and Jude
> On you I intrude
> By this paring I hold to discover,
> Without any delay,
> I pray you today,
> To tell me the name of my lover.[41]

The peeling was then thrown over the left shoulder, where
it was supposed to take on shape of the initial of the future
partner's surname. If no letter was clear, or it broke, it was
probable that the inquirer would not marry. However, if

every pip of the peeled apple was collected, put into a glass of water then drunk, the bad omen was cancelled out and another attempt the following year might bring better luck.

At Hallowe'en an apple peeling thrown over the left shoulder, to avoid the devil, was supposed to form a magical spiral and reveal the initial of a future husband or wife.[48] In some versions this had to take place at midnight.[50] A rhyme to accompany this went:

> I pare this pippin round and round again
> My sweetheart's name to flourish on the plain,
> I fling the unbroken paring o'er my head,
> My sweetheart's letter on the ground is read.[44]

An apple peel hung from the upper lintel of the door at Hallowe'en was thought to reveal the first names of future husbands and wives by noting the names of those who passed under it. The first male was supposed to have the name of the future husband of the oldest single female; the first female, the name of the future wife of the oldest single male present, and so on.[35] The apple peel could also be placed behind the door.[7]

CURES

Apples are associated with good health and healthy eating. They have been used in cures for many ailments. The most common one being for warts.

In Shropshire an apple was divided in two, one half was eaten, while the wart was rubbed with the other half, which was then thrown away.[51] Another version involves rubbing the wart with both halves, tying them together and burying the whole  thing. The wart would disappear as the buried fruit mould-ered away.[43] In Lincolnshire applying the juice was thought to remove them.

A cure for rheumatism or weakness of the eye was to apply a poultice made from rotten apples.[43]

Concoctions of fruit and blossoms have been used in beauty cultures, and were supposed to be especially effective in treating a red nose.[43]

Apple juice mixed with saffron is given for jaundice.[35]

A red rag soaked in verjuice (the juice of unripe apples, similar to vinegar) had a soothing effect on sore wrists suffered by harvesters each year before they became accustomed to the action of the scythe.[9]

In African American Folklore it was believed that apple shaped birth marks could be removed by rubbing them with the fruit and keeping the person on an apple diet. They were also used in voodoo love charms.[20]

SUPERSTITIONS

There are a great many magical beliefs about apples.
Cut an apple crossways and a five pointed star is revealed,
different for every variety of apple. This has been seen as a
pentagram, the ancient symbol of magic or protection. The
star is a symbol of guidance or hope for a better future. This
fits in with both the idea of apple bobbing, where you win
an apple and get good luck and health for the future year or
miss and get half drowned or hit by a flying apple or candle,
and using apples for fortune telling.[50]

To place a spell in the centre of an apple (in the stem) cut it
crossways, bury the fruit and when it disintegrates the spell
comes true. *June and Robin Small, Charlton Orchards, Somerset*

A woman was carrying her child along a road, the child was
eating an apple. They met another women who took the
apple from the child, bit a piece out of it and returned it to
him. His health, which had been good up until this point,
declined and eventually he died. *Shropshire* [43]

To eat an apple without rubbing it is to challenge the devil.
Surrey [21]

Thunder on Shrove Tuesday meant winds and a good fruit
crop to look foward to.[8]

To the Celts the apple symbolised immortality and the tree was their tree of paradise. Mystery plays of the Middle Ages always included a Garden of Eden play which was performed inside a ring of candles set round a fir tree hung with apples.[39]

In Devon apples were never picked during a waning moon in case they shrumped up, but in other parts of the country the opposite was believed and apples picked during the moon's increase would not keep.[35]

Hoard or keeping apples were picked in the moon's dark, lest harmful rays caused rot, but grafts were successful and fruit trees grew straighter if pruning and graffing were done at the increase.

From moon being
changed,
Till past be the prime,
For graffing and
cropping,
Is a very good time.[9]

If it is a good year for apples, it is a great year for twins.[48]

> If good apples you would have,
> The leaves must go into the grave.
> *Devon* [35]

On Scattering Day red apples were rolled for children.[38]

In Guernsey it was believed that watering the trees with urine made the apples sweeter.[9]

> Apples, pears, hawthorn - quick oak; set them at
> All-hallowtide and command them to prosper; set them at
> Candlemas and entreat them to grow.[35]

The apple tree stood for a symbol of plenty and destroying it was thought to upset the household's fortunes, therefore it should never be cut purposely for use as fire wood.[9]

The importance of cider meant that apple trees were regarded with great affection, even reverence, it was once thought tantamount to sacrilege to cut them down. It was believed in Herefordshire and other parts of the country that if an orchard was destroyed in order to plant a hop-yard, the latter would never pay the cost of cultivation. This was originally thought to be because of the apple's magical reputation, but there appears to be some truth in it.[43]

Throwing the afterbirth of cows into the branches of apple trees was thought to bring them fertility. [34]

If the first apple on a young tree was picked and eaten by a woman who had many children, then it too would have many fruitful seasons.[52]

Amulets or stones with holes through them were hung between apple trees to protect the orchard, they were also used in houses and cowsheds. *Frogham, Hampshire*[9]

Planting an apple tree on a piece of common land enclosed it and the lord of the manor kept his rights over the land by taking some of the fruit each year.[52]

A apple tree should not be planted near an ash or mountain ash (wicken) as one will kill the other.
Exmoor [12]

Apple blossom was considered to be an emblem of choice.[15]

Apple blossom was never taken inside, since it would bring sickness on the house.[9]

In Northamptonshire flowers and fruit together on a tree, which is not unusual, meant a death in the family.

> A bloom on the tree when apples are ripe,
> Is a sure termination of somebody's life.[8]

However in mainland Europe an apple tree blooming out of season meant the owner could expect good fortune.[52]

In Wales if a crab apple tree overhanging a well blossomed out of season it was believed that there would be more births and marriages than deaths that year.[48]

Dreaming about apples foretold a long life, sucess in trade and a lover's faithfulness, but it was a bad omen to dream about fruit or flowers out of season.

A Sussex saying:

> Fruit out of season,
> Sounds out of reason.[15]

To dream of fruit or any kind of crop during its proper season was an indication of good luck.

If an apple was left on the tree during the winter months and hung there until spring it was considered as an omen of death.[35]

In many parts of the country, however, it was considered lucky to leave an apple or two either on the ground or on the tree after the harvest, to keep any wandering spirits happy.[43] In Yorkshire a small apple was left as a propitiating gift and care was taken to thank the tree for its fruit.[52] In other parts of the country the small or damaged apples were left on the tree for the birds, who were the guardian spirits.[9] These apples were thought to be the property of the fairy folk, the piskie harvest. In the West Country children were once encouraged to steal these, probably to overcome the fact that if they were still there in the spring it was seen as unlucky. In the Cotswolds this was known as 'a-scraggling' and was referred to as this until the 1970's; in West Somerset as Pixying or Pisking; on the Blackdowns as Pixy-warding or Pixy-hoarding; in South Somerset as Cull-pixying and in East Somerset as Griggling.[43]

In Somerset Lazy Lawrence was seen as the spirit of

indolence and like the pony form of the colt-pixy, a guardian of the orchard. He stopped those who steal the griggling apples, as well as anyone trying to go about their work by transfixing them.

> Lazy Lawrence let me goo
> Don't hold me summer and winter too.[12]

Apples which had not fallen to the ground were pothered or ponked, shaken or knocked down, with long ash poles.[32] Dubbing was knocking these apples down by throwing sticks at them.[9]

REFERENCES

1. Jean Harrowven, Origins of Rhymes, Songs & Sayings, Kaye & Ward, 1977.
2. Peter Blackburne-Maze, The Apple Book, W.H.&L. Collingridge Ltd, 1986.
3. Iona & Peter Opie, The Lore & Language of School Children, Oxford University Press, 1959.
4. Amy Stewart Fraser, Dae Ye Min' Langsyne, Routledge & Kegan Paul, 1975.
5. Geoffrey Palmer & Noel Lloyd, A Year of Festivals, Warne, 1972.
6. Val Archer, A Basket of Apples, Pavilion, 1993.
7. Mrs. M. Macleod Banks, British Calendar Customs, Scotland, Folklore Society, 1941.
8. Wright & Lones, British Calendar Customs, England, Vol 1,2&3, Folklore Society, 1940.
9. Margaret Baker, Folklore & Customs of Rural England, David & Charles, 1974.
10. Elizabeth Ashford, What to do with an apple, Elizabeth Ashford, n.d.
11. Iona & Peter Opie, Childrens games in street & playground, Oxford University Press, 1979.
12. Ruth L. Tongue, Somerset Folklore, Folklore Society, 1965.
13. Pat Morris, Hedgehogs, Whittlet Press, 1983.
14. Jane Pettigrew, The Festive Table, Pavilion, 1993.
15. Richard Folkard, Plant Lore, legends & lyrics, ?London, 1884.
16. Miranda J. Green, Dictionary of Celtic Myth & Legend, Thames & Hudson, 1992.
17. Brewer's Dictionary of Phrases & Fables, Cassell, 1990.

18. Anne M. Avakian, "Three apples fell from heaven" - Armenian and Turkish Tales, Folklore Vol.98, 1987.

19. Herbert Spencer Robinson & Knox Wilson, Encyclopaedia of Myths & Legends of all Nations, Edmund Ward Ltd, 1962.

20. Funk & Wagnall's Standard Dictionary of Folklore, Mythology & Legend, Harper & Row, 1972.

21. Roy Palmer, Personal research, "Recital for Two Voices", 1993.

22. Bel Bailey, "Make the most of Apple Day - and tell your customers", British Baker, 26/9/92.

23. Iona & Peter Opie, The Oxford Nursery Rhyme Book, Oxford University Press, 1955.

24. Ruth L. Tongue, The Chime Child or Somerset Singers, Routledge & Kegan Paul, 1967.

25. D. Occomore & P. Stratley, Bushes & Briars, an anthology of Essex folksongs, Monkswood Press, 1979.

26. Toni Arthur, All the year round, a compendium of games, customs & stories, Puffin, 1981.

27. Chaundler, A year book of Folklore, Mowbray & Co., n.d.

28. Julian Franklyn, Dictionary of Rhyming Slang, Routledge & Kegan Paul, 1960.

29. Burton Egburt Stevenson, Stevenson's Book of Proverbs, Maxims & Familiar phrases, Routledge, 1949.

30. F. P. Wilson, Oxford Dictionary of English Proverbs, Oxford University Press, 1970.

31. Bartlett Jere Whiting, Proverbs, Sentences & Proverbial phrases, Oxford University Press, 1968.

32. Whiting's Proverbs, Sentences & Proverbial phrases, Harvard University Press, 1968.

33. J.A. Simpson, Concise Oxford Dictionary of Proverbs, Oxford University Press, 1982.

34. Roy Palmer, The Folklore of Hereford & Worcester, Logaston Press, 1992.

35. Thomas F. Thiselton Dyer, The Folklore of Plants, Singing Tree Press, 1968.

36. Robert L. Chapman, New Dictionary of American Slang, Macmillan, 1986.

37. Robert L. Chapman, Thesaurus of American Slang, Harper & Row, 1989.

38. Carpenter Collection, Reel 1, English Folk Dance & Song Society.

39. Elizabeth Luard, European Festival Foods, Bantam, 1990.

40. Julia Jones & Barbara Deer, Cattern Cakes & Lace, Dorling Kindersley, 1987.

41. Ruth Ward, A Harvest of Apples, Penguin, 1988.

42. E. F. Coote Lake, "Folklife & Traditions", Folklore vol.77, 1966.

43. Christina Hole, Encyclopaedia of Superstitions, Hutchinson, 1961.

44. Christina Hole, British Folk Customs, Hutchinson, 1976.

45. Chris Morris, Gloucestershire Folklore, Gloucester Folk Museum, 1988.

46. Plough Monday, Education Series pack no. 2, English Folk Dance & Song Society, 1991.

47. Trevor M. Owen, Welsh Folk Customs, Welsh Folk Museum, 1978.

48. Iona Opie & Moira Tatem, Dictionary of Superstitions, Oxford University Press, 1989.

49. Brian Bonnard, Channel Island Plant Lore, Brian Bonnard, 1993.

50. Marian Green, A Calendar of Festivals, Element, 1991.

51. Charlotte Sophia Burne, Shropshire Folklore, E.P. Publications Ltd, 1973.

52. Phillippa Waring, Dictionary of Omens and Superstitions, Souvenir Press, 1978.

FURTHER READING

Henry M. Belden & Arthur Palmer Hudson, The Frank C. Browns Collection of North Carolina, vol III, folksongs from North Carolina, Duke University Press, 1952.

Briggs & Tongue, Folktales of England, University of Chicago Press, 1965.

Steve Berry, Apples - An educational project for 7-11 year olds, Educational Project Resources, n.d.

Bertrand Harris Bronson, Traditional Tunes of the Child Ballads, Princetown University Press, 1959.

Italo Calvino, Italian Folktales, Penguin, 1956.

Michael Dames, Mythic Ireland, Thames & Hudson, 1972.

Joe Durham, The Farming Game, Women's Farming Union, 1991.

Peter Berresford-Ellis, Dictionary of Celtic Mythology, Constable, 1922.

Alice Gomme, Traditional Games of England, Scotland & Ireland, Thames & Hudson, 1984.

Reg Hall, I never played too many posh dances - Scan Tester, Sussex musician 1887-1972, Musical Traditions, 1990.

Margaret Hannagan & Seamus Clandillon, Songs of the Irish Gaels, Oxford University Press, 1927.

E. F. Coote Lake, "Folklife & Traditions", Folklore vol. 70, 1959.

Elizabeth Lamb, Cornish Wassailing Today, English Dance & Song, Winter/Christmas, 1969.

Ella Mary Leather, Folklore of Herefordshire, S.R. Publishers Ltd, 1970.

Ledbury Reporter, "There's not a single demon in the orchard", 15/1/93.

Barbara Leonie-Picard, French Legends, Tales & Fairy Stories, Oxford University Press, Picard, 1955.

Alan Lomax, The folksongs of North America, Cassell, 1960.

Alton C. Morris, Folksongs of Florida, Folklorica, 1991.

Iona & Peter Opie, The Singing Game, Oxford University Press, 1985.

Iona & Peter Opie, Oxford Dictionary of Nursery Rhymes, Oxford University Press, 1951.

Elizabeth Poston, The Second Penguin Book of Christmas Carols, Penguin, 1970.

James Riordan, Tales from Central Russia (book 1), Kestrel, 1976.

Dorothy Spicer, Festivals of Western Europe, HW Wilson & Co, 1958.

Charles Squire, Celtic Myth & Legend, Poetry & Romance, Gresham Publishing Co, n.d.

GOOD APPLE BOOKS

John Bultitude, Apples: a guide to the identification of international varieties, Macmillan Reference Books, 1983.

Common Ground, The Apple Source Book: particular recipes for diverse apples, Common Ground, 1991.

Common Ground, Orchards: a guide to local conservation, Common Ground, 1989.

Joan Morgan & Alison Richards, The Book of Apples, Ebury Press, 1993.

F.A. Roach, Cultivated Fruits of Britain, Basil Blackwell, 1985.

Rosanne Sanders, The English Apple, Phaidon Press 1988.

FORMAL ACKNOWLEDGEMENTS

Toni Arthur, All the Year Round, Puffin, 1981. © Toni Arthur 1979. Reproduced by permission of Curtis Brown, London Ltd.

Margaret Baker, Folklore and Customs of Rural England, David and Charles, 1974. By permission.

Amy Stewart Fraser, Dae Ye Min Langsyne, Routledge and Kegan Paul, 1975. By permission.

Chris Morris, GloucestershireFolk Lore,Gloucestershire Folk Museum, 1988. By permission.

Peter and Iona Opie, The Lore and Language of School Children, 1959, by permission of Oxford University Press.

Peter and Iona Opie, The Oxford Nursery Rhyme Book, 1955, by permission of Oxford University Press.

Iona Opie and Moira Tatem, The Dictionary of Superstitions, 1989, by permission of Oxford University Press.

Jane Pettigrew, The Festive Table, Pavilion, 1990. By permission.

J. A. Simpson, Concise Oxford Dictionary of English Proverbs, 1982, by permission of Oxford University Press.

Ruth L. Tongue, Somerset Folklore, Folklore Society, 1965.

Ruth L. Tongue, The Chime Child or Somerset Singers, Routledge and Kegan Paul, 1967. Acknowledgement the copyright holder, Mrs M. M. Stone, and the Folklore Society.

Whiting's Proverbs, Sentences and Proverbial Phrases, Harvard University Press, 1968, reprinted by permission of Harvard University Press. © Harvard University Press.

F. P. Wilson, The Oxford Dictionary of English Proverbs, 1970, by permission of Oxford University Press.

Wright and Lones, British Calendar Customs: England vols 1,2,3, Folklore Society, 1940. All material appears by courtesy of the Folklore Society.

CALENDAR
Days mentioned in the text

JANUARY
1st - New Year's Day
5th - Twelfth Night
6th - Twelfth Day
18th - Old Twelfth Night
FEBRUARY
14th - St Valentine's Day
Collop Monday
Shrove Tuesday
Fritter or Ash Wednesday
MARCH/APRIL
Easter Sunday
Easter Monday
MAY
Rogation Week (5th Sunday after Easter)
Ascentiontide
19th - St Dunstan's Day
JUNE
23rd - Midsummer's Eve/St John's Eve
24th - St John's Day
29th - St Peter's Day
JULY
15th - St Swithin's Day
17th - St Kenelm's Day
25th - St James' Day
First Sunday after 28th - Kenelm's Wake
AUGUST
25th - Apple Pie Fair, Marldon, Devon

SEPTEMBER
1st - St Giles' Day
First Sunday after St Giles' Day - Revel Sunday
14th -Holy-Rood or Holy-Cross Day
Sunday following Holy-Rood Day - Pig Face Sunday
18th - Cumberland Crab Fair
19th - Nativity of the Virgin Mary
29th - Michaelmas Day
OCTOBER
11th - Old Michaelmas Day
18th - St Luke's Day
21st - Apple Day
28th - Feast of St Simon and St Jude
31st - Hallowe'en
NOVEMBER
1st - All Saints' or All Hallows' Day
2nd - All Souls' Day
5th - Bonfire Night
23rd - St Clement's Day
24th - St Catherine's Eve
25th - St Catherine's Day
30th - St Andrew's Night
DECEMBER
20th - St Thomas' Eve
21st - St Thomas' Day
24th - Christmas Eve
25th Christmas Day
31st - New Year's Eve

JANE'S APPLE LIST

APPLE HEADED PUPPETS
Probably most round cooking apples would be big enough, but some go soft as they get older so best to use them early in the season. Suggested varieties: Grenadier, Bramley, Alfriston, Annie Elizabeth (used by the Victorians for dining-table displays), Ashmeads Kernel (smaller dessert variety but late keeping, so firm), Howgate Wonder, Warners King, Reverend Wilks, Ribston Pippin (late keeping dessert), Newton Wonder, Dumelow's Seedling (Wellington), Lane's Prince Albert, Norfolk Biffin.

SMALL APPLES
Lots of the older varieties or older trees produce small fruit and many fruit farms sell these at a cheaper price, others which have a tendency to be small are: Discovery, Devonshire Quarrenden, St Edmunds Pippin, Merton Beauty, Sunset, Margil, Fiesta, Lord Burghley, Tydeman's Late Orange, Pitmaston Pine Apple, Baker's Delicious.

APPLE HOG
Apples similar to those suggested for puppets would be suitable, but perhaps better to have large dessert rather than cookers, such as: Gascoyne's Scarlet, Suntan, Blenheim Orange, Orleans Reinette, Laxton's Superb, Cornish Gilliflower, Belle de Boskoop, Claygate Pearmain, Brownlees' Russet, King's Acre Pippin.

APPLE DAY

Common Ground is working to encourage people to value and enjoy their own familiar surroundings. We chose the apple as a symbol of the variety that we are losing in almost everything around us. If we lose the orchard we lose not only genetic variety, but also a way of life, the words that are associated with the locality, the songs, the look and feel of the place. We impoverish our cultural landscape.

Apple Day is celebrated locally throughout the country on October 21st, or the nearest weekend to it, to help make apparent the links between the apple and your landscape. Local ways of celebrating fruit may already exist, these may be worth reinventing if they are no longer practised. Apple Games and Customs is full of ideas, others follow - but you can start with an apple supper at home:

- Encourage local shops to stock local varieties for the day (and subsequently).
- Collect information for a local fruit recipe book or pamphlet - publish it and launch it with an orchard feast.
- Excite local pubs and restaurants to excel themselves with special menus and guest ciders.
- Encourage local horticultural societies and gardeners to give grafting and pruning demonstrations and run a swap shop.
- Add a new dimension to your autumn coffee morning; prepare a fruit feast and organise displays, tastings or competitions of local food and drink.
- Organise an Apple Roadshow. Use local experts to help people to identify the varieties of apple in their garden and to diagnose

any disease which may be afflicting them.
- Celebrate wild fruits. Make a map of the wild crab apple, cherry, bullace, sloe and others, make sure they are cared for in hedgerow, garden and wood.
-Research and revive local traditions about orchards and apples.
-Organise an exhibition of photographs by local people of local orchards and portraits of fruit trees - domestic and wild.
- Organise orchard visits,walks and picnics.
- Run an Apple Hunt. Find out what apple varieties the locality has in its gardens and orchards, encourage their care.
- Organise wild life and mistletoe surveys in orchards.

SAVE OUR ORCHARDS

Why Conserve Old Orchards?

Orchards are important for many reasons:
- they create beautiful landscapes;
- fruit trees are a source of good food - from apple pie to cider
- they can be valuable habitats for wild life and wild flowers, bees love fruit blossom and blossom needs bees;
- orchards and fruit trees are a rich source of poetic inspiration;
- locally grown fruit provides local jobs and reduces transport costs - and pollution;
- old varieties of fruit and wild fruit trees are irreplaceable sources of genetic diversity and may be or may parent the disease resistant strains of tomorrow;
- orchards have a long tradition of multiple use - as places to graze sheep, geese and pigs, for the production of honey and as delightful places in which to stroll and rest;

- they are imbued with local cultural significance. With communal effort, imagination and a little money, they can again become a valuable asset to the locality.

What To Do - New Life for Old Varieties

There are many ways in which we can begin to care for old orchards and fruit trees.

1) Find out what you have. Are there any orchards in your neighbourhood or parish? Are there many fruit trees growing in local gardens? Where are they and who is responsible for them?

2) Start a parish apple register or orchard map - noting the different varieties that grow in gardens, orchards and hedgerows. Record the area, condition and number of trees. Search for varieties that are particular to your locality.

3) Trace the origins of varieties - especially those which have local associations. You might even discover a long lost variety. Get a copy of Common Ground's Apple Map and county gazetteer. The Brogdale Trust (Faversham, Kent) and Royal Horticultural Society (Wisley, Surrey) offer a fruit identification service.

4) Campaign to save local orchards and fruit trees which are threatened by development. They are frequently undervalued by planners and farmers. Propose alternative uses - why not establish a community orchard?

5) Talk to the local farmer or grower. Find out if they have any

old orchards that they are prepared to let or sell to the local community to care for and renovate. Contact the Countryside Commission, and your County or District Council about grants.

6) Encourage the retention, planting and care of wild and cultivated fruit trees in hedgerows.

7) Encourage local commercial orchards to open, for visits, purchase and to taste the fruit. Visit the nearest 'Pick Your Own' orchard, suggest they initiate a 'rent-a-tree' scheme involving families and schools. Encourage them to grow local varieties and hold events.

8) Grow local varieties of fruit in your own garden. Consult growers and gardeners about varieties of fruit particular to your area. Take care to choose appropriate pollinators. Plant trees between November and March. Take grafts from your favourite old trees - it's not as difficult as it might at first seem.

9) Encourage shops to sell a wider range of local fruit and fruit products. Drink cider made from British cider apples and perry from perry pears - obtain a copy of the 'Good Cider Guide' published by the Campaign for Real Ale. Rediscover and create recipes using local varieties of fruit.

10) Set up a community orchard, re-establish a city orchard or create a school orchard. Encourage your local council to plant fruit trees on public land, in a corner of the park, on new estates, and on the edge of the town or city.

11) Celebrate Apple Day on October 21st.

ABOUT COMMON GROUND

Creating the circumstances for local knowledge and professional expertise to inform each other, Common Ground pioneers imaginative ways of reweaving the local world. We try to inspire people to join in the exploration of the richness in everyday places, popular culture, common wild life, ordinary buildings and landscapes, to revalue our emotional engagement with places and all that they mean to us and to go on to become actively involved in their care.

LOCAL DISTINCTIVENESS

We are all familiar with where we live and work, we take it for granted, but its significance lies in its very ordinariness to us. We understand a place in close up, the details spark the telling of stories, act as lightning conductors for both arousing curiosity and passing on knowledge.

This web of rich understandings between people and the land, people and their histories, is not about scenery, it takes us below the surface, to where the land might reflect back to us purpose and belonging. Local Distinctiveness is about what small places mean to us, their authenticity, detail, patina and identity. It involves everywhere. Understanding what makes our place different from the next, what accumulations of story upon history upon natural history give it its uniqueness may help us to maintain a relationship which ensures a future for the richness of locality.

WEBSITES & PUBLICATIONS

The Common Ground Book of Orchards, Common Ground 2000, (£25.00 incl p&p) 224 pages, fully illustrated and with over 120 photographs, 27 in colour and 50 by James Ravilious

The Apple Source Book, particular recipes for diverse apples, Common Ground, 1991/4

Apple Day and Parish Maps leaflets, free with an sae

Save our Orchards, Community Orchards pamphlets

The Apple Map fully illustrated with lists of varieties of apples county by county, (colour Al poster)

Apple Day postcard, one of a set of six calendar festival cards.

Apple postcards, 12 varieties and one composite, watercolours by Charles Raymond

The Apple Broadcast, Common Ground, 1994, 16 page A3 newspaper

Trees Be Company: a poetry anthology edited by Angela King and Sue Clifford for Common Ground, Green Books, 2001

Common Ground Rules for Local Distinctiveness - an ABC of the locally particular from Ayrshire Cows to Zennor Church, (illustrated broadsheet/poster, A2)

Available from:
Common Ground, Gold Hill House, 21 High Street, Shaftesbury, Dorset SP7 8JE

For an up to date list of Common Ground publications and prices send an A5 SAE or see websites: www.commonground.org.uk and www.england-in-particular.info for philosophy, campaigning, events and publications information

Trade orders to Worldly Goods 0117 942 0165